GW00818710

The Complete Proficiency Practice Tests

1

Peter May

Introduction to the examination by Simon Greenall

HEINEMANN

Heinemann International Publishing
a division of Heinemann Publishers (Oxford) Ltd
Halley Court, Jordan Hill, Oxford OX2 8EJ

OXFORD   LONDON   EDINBURGH
MELBOURNE   SYDNEY   AUCKLAND
IBADAN   NAIROBI   GABORONE
HARARE   PORTSMOUTH (USA)
SINGAPORE   MADRID   ATHENS   BOLOGNA

ISBN 0 435 28805 9

© Peter May   Simon Greenall 1990
All rights reserved; no part of this publication may be reproduced, stored in a retrieval system, or
transmitted in any form or by any means, electronic, mechanical, photocopying, recording, or
otherwise, without the prior written permission of the Publishers.

First published 1990

Cassettes produced by James Richardson at Studio AVP
Designed by Chris Bell
Cover design by Mike Brain
Illustrated by Maddie Baker, Tim Beer and Oxprint Illustrators

Typeset by Tradespools Ltd, Frome, Somerset
Printed and bound in Great Britain by
M & A Thomson Litho Ltd, East Kilbride, Scotland
91 92 93 94 10 9 8 7 6 5 4 3 2

CONTENTS

ACKNOWLEDGEMENTS

The author wishes to thank the following for their help: the students, teachers and library resources staff of the British Council evening school in Madrid, Bill Anderson, Jill Florent and Karen Jacobs of Heinemann International, and Herme.

The author and publishers would like to thank the following people for their help: Examiners Karen Giblin, Katy Shaw, Ian Thompson and Ken Wilford; Pam Murphy, staff and students at Godmer House, Oxford; Peter Hill and students at Kilburn College, London; Clare West and students at the English Language Centre, Hove; Students at the school of Ms. Stamatiou, Theodoropoulou, Athens; William Paterson and Jacky Newbrook.

We would like to thank the following for permission to reproduce copyright material: Sir David Attenborough, 'How Unnatural is TV Natural History?' (p. 83); The British Broadcasting Corporation, 'In a Nutshell' by Christopher Nicholson (p. 20), 'New Ideas' by Peter Goodwin (p. 21), 'In Other Words' (p. 22), 'The Sixties' by Janice Winship (p. 63); Epson UK Ltd, 'Just because you're small, it doesn't mean you can't be powerful' (p. 70); Guardian, 'Desk Top Crooks' by Robert Goodwins (p. 30), 'Rats in the Sudan' by Stephen Cook (p. 83); Guardian News Service Ltd, 'Blue Skies Up Above' by Dick File (p. 60); Guardian Weekly, 'The Waking Nightmare' by Sally Stucke (p. 10), various extracts (p. 45), 'Travellers to an Undiscovered Country' by Geoffrey Taylor (p. 11), 'Book review' by Christine Koning (p. 45), 'Dicing with Danger, Madrid Diary' by John Hooper (p. 25), 'Jungle Warfare' by Polly Toynbee (p. 55), 'The Dank Outsider' Jane Ellison (p. 75), 'Fat-free Fat is Food for Thought' by James Erlichman (p. 73), 'Time to Call it a Day' by Simon Winchester (p. 66). The Independent, 'Watchdog on Broadcasting' by Michael Leapman (p. 61), 'Old Pop Hits Top the Charts' by John Windsor (p. 59), 'Time to Play a More Populist Tune' by Dave Hill (p. 45), 'Disaster on a Major Scale' by Mark Lawson (p. 50), 'Around the World's Oceans in 265 Days' by Stuart Alexander (p. 58). Jackie Magazine, D.C Thomson & Co Ltd, 'He's making a fool of her' and 'Keeping it secret' from Cathy and Claire page (p. 63). The Listener, 'Lost sessions and sticky tapes, by Ken Garner (p. 37). New Statesman and Society, 'Thatcher's Untouchables' by Claire Saunders (p. 41). Newsweek, 'The Sweet uses of duty free liquor' by Phillip Jacobson (p. 51). New Scientist, 'Why Scientists keep it obscure' by Ted Nields (p. 28), 'Letter Page' by Ella Van Eddajk (p. 51), 'Warning, snoring can damage your health' by Jim Horne (p. 32). The Observer, 'Gold Rush at Fever Pitch' by Juliet Rix (p. 79), 'Street Whys' by Jonathon Sale (p. 43). Penguin Books, 'The Conger Eel' (extract p. 83). Space Time Publications Ltd. 1988. Extracted from, 'A brief history of time' published by Bantam Press, a division of Transworld Publishers Ltd (p. 68). All rights reserved. The Spectator, 'Danger from little green men' by Adrian Berry, Science Correspondent of the Daily Telegraph (p. 42), 'The lead balloon goes up' by Des Wilson (p. 25), 'Nuclear Power? Yes Please' by Andrew Kenny (p. 40). Sunday Telegraph Ltd., 'Home is where the hype is' by Brenda Maddox (p. 48). 'A work out for the jams' by Colin Dryden (p. 25), 'Sober and Out' by Paul Keers (p. 51). Times Newspapers Ltd., 'On the Edge' by Roger Ratcliffe (p. 17), 'Get with the beat and snore no more' by Philip Beresford (p. 32), 'Another day, another dolour' by Penny Mayrick (p. 12), 'Drunk as a Lord on tonics' by Ian Smith (p. 51), 'How to jump queue fury' by John S. Wilson (p. 78), 'Mobile phones...' by Valerie Elliot (p. 80).

While every effort has been made to trace the owners of copyright material in this book, there have been cases where the publishers have been unable to locate the sources. We would be grateful to hear from anyone who recognises their copyright material and who is unacknowledged.

Photographs acknowledgements: Camera Press (p. 44), Greg Evans Picture Library (p. 82) and Zefa Photo Library (p. 24, 44, 62 and 82).

THE CERTIFICATE OF PROFICIENCY

THE EXAMINATION PAPERS

The Certificate of Proficiency in English has five papers:

Paper 1: Reading Comprehension (1 hour)
Section A 25 multiple choice questions which test your vocabulary and grammar. One mark is given for each correct answer.

Section B 15 multiple choice questions about three or more passages which test how well you understand the general sense, specific information, inference, style, register and the writer's intention.

In all there are 55 marks which are scaled down to 40.

Paper 2: Composition (2 hours)
Two compositions from a choice of five topics. You have to write about 350 words for each composition. On a task-based exercise you may be asked for two pieces of about 150 words each. Writing about the set texts is optional.

   The paper tests how well you use language naturally and extensively in response to various themes or situations. Fluency, accuracy and fulfilment of the task set are three of the most important marking criteria.

There are 40 marks for this paper. Each essay is marked out of 20.

Paper 3: Use of English (2 hours)
A variety of exercises to test use of the language.

Section A The exercises in this section usually include a blank filling activity which concentrates on structure, sentence transformation, a blank filling activity which concentrates on vocabulary and a rewriting task based on a single word stimulus.

Section B This section consists of a passage to test reading comprehension and summary skills. There are usually a number of short answer questions, and a summary writing task in which you have to summarise the main points of the passage in a given number of words.

There may be 70 or more items in this paper, but the marks are scaled down to 40.

Paper 4: Listening Comprehension (about 30 minutes)
A number of questions of different types which test how well you understand three to five authentic or simulated texts. The paper tests not only your comprehension of the main ideas or specific information but also your ability to interpret the speakers' attitudes through the stress and intonation patterns. Because the passages may be from an authentic source, there may be some background noise. It is likely to be distracting at first, but you will get used to it.

Paper 5: Interview (about 15–20 minutes)
To start the interview, the examiner will show you a picture and will ask you to describe what you see. Next the examiner will show you a short passage which could be something said by someone in the picture you have seen, or by someone looking at the picture. The examiner will ask you who is speaking, where the text comes from, who it was written for, etc*. Finally, you will be asked to take part in a discussion or a communication activity based on the general theme of the interview, often using authentic material. However, if you want to, you can talk about the set texts during this final part.

   More and more people are doing this paper in groups of two or three. But remember, it's you who chooses. Ask your teacher for advice.

   This paper tests six aspects of your ability to speak English: your fluency, grammatical accuracy, pronunciation of sounds, pronunciation of sentences, how well you communicate and your range of vocabulary. Each aspect has up to 6 marks, making 30 in all. This mark is scaled up to 40, so that it has equal importance with Papers 1, 2 and 3.

   Papers 1, 2 and 3 usually take place either on the same day or on consecutive days. Paper 4 and Paper 5 may take place before or after Papers 1, 2 and 3 because of the special arrangements required to administer these papers.

*It is possible that this part of the exam will be changed in the near future. If it is, your teacher will be informed.

HOW THE EXAMINATION IS MARKED

When you get your result, you will get a grade A, B or C which is a pass, D or E, which is a fail. At the moment, the Examination Syndicate does not usually give details concerning your performance on individual papers, although for failed candidates it indicates which papers did not reach the required level. However, it may be possible in the future to obtain your paper-by-paper results, although this will not change the overriding principle of the examination being a balanced test of your language skill.

Papers 2 and 5 are marked by examiners. The mark they give you for one paper will be checked against the marks given to you in other papers. If these marks are not more or less the same, then your performance will be looked at more closely to make sure that no examiner has given you a mark that does not relate to your overall performance. The examiner's performance is also compared with all the other examiners, so that these subjective parts of the examination are as fair as possible. For more information about the marking scales used, please see page 5.

QUESTIONS AND ANSWERS ABOUT THE CERTIFICATE OF PROFICIENCY

Here are the answers to some questions which candidates have often asked.

What's the pass mark for the exam?

The pass mark for the exam changes each time. A day or so after the examination, a group of examiners, who know the standard very well, meet to decide if the exam is more or less difficult than usual. They then decide what the pass mark will be and each candidate's marks are adjusted accordingly. However, you can expect a grade C pass if you get 22–25 marks (about 60%) in Paper 1, 16 out of 40 (ie. 8 out of 20 for each composition, about 40%) in Paper 2, and 3 out of 5 on each of the marking scales in Paper 5 (remember that the total of 30 is scaled up to 40). It is more difficult to say how many marks would give a grade C for Papers 3 and 4 because the total number of items varies from exam to exam, but you should aim for about 60% in each case.

Why do so many people fail Proficiency?

It is a demoralising fact for both candidates and teachers that in any year more people fail than pass. The reason for this is that the examination is a very broad ranging test of a candidate's ability in English. The extent of structures and vocabulary is too great to define accurately, and to a certain extent it must be said that the examination tests skills, such as ordering, presenting and interpreting information or the successful realisation of specific tasks, in which a candidate may be deficient in his or her own language. It is not just a test of what English you have learnt or acquired, it is also a test of how well you can communicate in an English-speaking environment. Perhaps most important, the gap between the First Certificate in English examination which you may have taken, and Proficiency may be greater than you or your teacher imagines. But it is important for you to know that there is no policy by the Examination Syndicate to fail a given number or percentage of candidates each year. And remember that plenty of people pass as well!

Is the December examination harder?

This is the most common question about the perceived level of the examination. Other variations are, 'is the June examination harder?' or 'why is Proficiency getting more and more difficult?

The level required does not change, although inevitably because different passages and questions are used each time, the exam may sometimes appear more or less difficult than usual. Earlier it was mentioned that examiners meet to discuss the relative difficulty of each paper, and if necessary, the marks at the lower and upper limits of each grade are adjusted. So, if a paper is considered to be difficult by the examiners, the pass mark is lowered, so that the overall requirement remains the same.

Is there more than one answer to multiple choice questions?

No. If you're wrong you get no marks, but you don't lose marks for wrong answers. It is also important to know that all items, such as multiple choice questions are pre-tested to make sure that they can be answered fairly and that they discriminate fairly between strong and weak candidates.

What's the examiner looking for in Paper 2?

He or she will be checking how well you perform the task set, how varied and appropriate your language is, and how correct your grammar, spelling and punctuation is. But where Proficiency differs from First Certificate is in the content of your composition; you should show some breadth of experience or background knowledge of the themes you choose. Nevertheless, a lively, imaginative, but grammatically faulty composition will not necessarily get more marks than a dull but accurate one. Try not to be irrelevant; each word in the question set is carefully chosen, and you should take equal care in answering it. This is important because it stops people being given credit for including material which is learnt by heart. If an examiner sees that you have not answered the question, he or she may decide to mark your composition out of 15 rather than 20.

If you write more in Paper 2 and Paper 3 part B, do you get more marks?

You may do, if your composition is excellent and to the point without becoming repetitive. But don't forget that if you write too much you may make more mistakes. Similarly, if you write less than the number of words specified, this won't automatically count against you if the composition is a successful realisation of the task set. The number of words specified is intended as a guide only. Find out before the exam how many words you can write on a sheet of A4 paper: don't waste time in the exam counting the number of words for the sake of the examiner.

In the short answers of Paper 3 part B, the number of lines gives an indication of how much is expected. In the summary, it is very important to keep to the 70–90 word limit.

How are Paper 2 and Paper 3 part B marked?

With great care. First, the chief examiner for each paper meets with team leaders to ensure a common standard. Then the compositions are sent in batches to teams of examiners in Britain. The examiners are also shown a sample of marks given by their team leader to a typical answer to each question, usually within the *pass* and *good* parts of the marking scale (see page 5). They then mark a few compositions and send their marked scripts to the team leader. Next, they begin marking their first batch of 50 scripts. While they are doing this, they receive a note from the team leader advising them if they are marking high or low; if so, they must adjust the marks given so far. They then take out ten or so scripts from their first batch showing a broad range of the marks given, and send them to the team leader, who checks to see if they have adjusted their marking; once again, if they have not, they have to re-mark their scripts so far. This process continues with every batch of scripts. If an examiner is new to marking Proficiency, he or she sends all the marked scripts to a third person, known as a checker, who checks that the marks given are fair. When the team leader has finalised the marks with the examiners, he or she then co-ordinates the marks with the chief examiner, once again adjusting them if necessary. Finally, the mark is compared with the candidate's performance elsewhere in the exam, and if it is exceptional in any way, further adjustments can be made. It is in this final stage that the idea of the examination being a test of language competence rather than discrete skills is maintained.

The whole process is long and complicated. It is certainly subjective, but all the examiners are using the same marking scales and the same criteria, and the result is a fair as it can be.

Is there more than one correct answer in the Paper 3 blank filling passage?

There may be, but either correct answer will get the mark.

Everyone says the Listening passages in Paper 4 are very difficult. Is this true?

They are certainly examples of natural English and are not graded in any way for the non-native speaker. In real-life, people don't speak as clearly as one imagines, and there may be background noise to distract you. But by this time, you will have listened to a lot of authentic English in preparation for the examination and as part of an ordinary language course. You are unlikely to encounter anything which is intrinsically more difficult than anything you have heard so far in your studies or in real-life. What makes it difficult is the fact that you are doing an examination, and you're nervous. The acoustic conditions of the classroom where you take the paper may not be the best, and if this is the case, don't waste time: tell the person in charge that you can't hear and he or she will allow you to move to a better position. Remember also that you will hear each passage twice; it is always difficult to understand what is happening when you are dropped into the middle of a conversation, so listen carefully for the recorded description of the context, and look at the question paper for further clues. And remember that everyone finds this paper difficult!

Who are the interviewers for Paper 5?
Usually they are native English speakers, teachers of English as a foreign language who are highly experienced in the level required for Proficiency. They are not allowed to examine any of their own students or anyone they know. They are very conscious that the interview makes candidates even more nervous than other papers in the examination, and will do their best to put you at your ease, or will take your nervousness into account, as long as it does not affect your communication skills. And don't forget that the examiner's own performance is checked as well. The marks they give you are checked against the marks you get for the other papers; all your marks should be roughly similar. If you perform badly on one paper, such as the interview, and well in others, it will not mean complete disaster for you!

What are they looking for in Paper 5?
You can see the six criteria of the marking scales on page 5. They expect you to talk clearly and coherently and to perform well in discussions. Try not to give simple answers; talk at length in reply to questions, if possible.

What are the advantages of doing the Interview in groups?
Firstly, it is a more realistic test of your oral ability. Secondly, it allows the interviewer more time to listen and examine you. Sometimes there is an interviewer who asks the questions and keeps the interview going, and an examiner who judges how well you answer and interract with the group. Lastly, it may be comforting to do part of your exam with friends whom you can trust. Don't worry about the others talking too much. It is the interviewer's job to make sure this does not happen. And even if it does, he or she will certainly have got a good impression of your level. One final point: a group interview does not take two or three times as long as an individual interview. In the twenty minutes of a group interview, the examiner will still have enough time to make up his or her mind about you.

Is there any advantage in answering questions on the set texts?
You have the option of writing about them in Paper 2 and talking about them in paper 5. It is important to show that you have read them, and although the examiners are not looking for sophisticated literary analysis, you should show some detailed knowledge about them. If you did prepare the set texts, they would certainly give you some ideas for the content of your composition or interview. By the way, if you choose to answer questions on the set texts in one paper, you don't have to answer them in the other.

What about American English?
American English and other standard 'Englishes' are quite acceptable in written or spoken form, although it is important to be consistent.

Why does it take so long to get my result?
Partly because so many people take the examination, and partly because the marking process is so complicated in order to ensure a fair result.

What should I do if my result is not as good as expected?
First of all, discuss it with your teacher. If you both agree that you expected to do better, he or she can write to the Examination Syndicate in Cambridge asking for an explanation. Very occasionally, mistakes can happen and at the very least, your results will be looked at again. but the marking and checking process is as fair as it can be, and unfortunately, disappointing results may be due to a misunderstanding of the level required. Keep trying!

SAMPLE COMPOSITIONS AND INTERVIEWS

Proficiency paper 2

There are some sample compositions at the back of this book, or you can look at your own or your classmates' compositions. The examiners use the marking scales below to decide what mark to give each candidate.

Marking

	Language	Content	Background Texts (set books)
16–20	Ambitious in concept and approach, with high quality language use. Occasional native-speaker-type lapses.		**13–20** Interpretative in approach. Credit given for breadth, development and relevance of argument, appropriateness of illustration and quotation.
11–15	Natural and appropriate in style with only occasional errors. Some sophistication of language use.	Well-developed realisation of the task.	
8–10	Structure and usage communicated in a clear but limited manner.	Task reasonably attempted.	**9–12** Limited to a straight-forward narrative treatment. Credit given for clarity, organisation, and appropriate selection of material.
5–7	Lack of control/ numerous errors.	Topic area neither extended nor explored.	**1–7** Irrelevant, undirected and fails to demonstrate knowledge or understanding of the text.
1–4	Errors and narrowness of vocabulary prevent communication.	Gross irrelevance and/or too short for judgment to be formed.	

What additional considerations are there?

a The five questions provide five different tasks, each of which demands varying responses and techniques.

b The quality of the composition must be assessed as a fulfilment of the task set: its relevance and reorganisation as a whole and in terms of individual paragraphs.

c The quality of language used must be considered: the range and appropriateness of vocabulary and sentence structure; the correctness of grammatical usage, punctuation and spelling.

d The candidate's ability to display a breadth of experience or background knowledge and his or her use of illustration and allusion should be demonstrated.

e The balancing of accuracy and imagination must be achieved: to give equitable treatment of compositions which are pedestrian but accurate and those which are less accurate but which show greater qualities of liveliness and imagination.

Proficiency paper 5

Listen to the sample interviews on cassette 2. Use the marking scales to decide what mark to give each candidate.

1 Fluency

> 5 Virtually native-speaker speed and rhythm, and coherent presentation of thoughts, in all contexts.
>
> 4 Foreign, but with minimal hesitation in all contexts.
>
> 3 Minimal hesitation in everyday contexts, but some hesitation when discussing more abstract topics, though not such as to demand unreasonable patience of the listener.
>
> 2 Hesitation not unreasonable in everyday contexts, but impedes understanding on more abstract topics.
>
> 1 Speaks haltingly even in everyday contexts.
>
> 0 Not capable of connected speech.

2 Grammatical accuracy

5 Virtually native-speaker accuracy over a wide range of structures and in all contexts. Few if any errors of any kind.
4 Few errors even in complex structures when discussing abstract topics. No basic errors.
3 Structures adequately controlled and varied in most contexts. Few if any basic errors.
2 Structures adequate in everyday contexts but limited in range and with basic errors not infrequent.
1 Frequent basic errors.
0 No awareness of basic grammatical functions.

3 Pronunciation: Sentences

5 Virtually native-speaker stress-timing, rhythm and placing of stress, intonation patterns and range of pitch within sentence; natural linking of phrases.
4 Stress-timing, rhythm, placing of stress, intonation, etc. sufficiently native-like as to make comprehension easy and listening pleasurable.
3 Stress-timing, rhythm, placing of stress, intonation, etc. sufficiently controlled.
2 Foreign speech patterns make the candidate occasionally difficult to understand.
1 Foreign speech patterns severely impede comprehension.
0 Not intelligible, through faulty stress and intonation.

4 Pronunciation: Individual sounds

5 All individual sounds virtually as a native speaker.
4 Most individual sounds virtually at native-speaker level.
3 All sounds sufficiently correct to be understood without difficulty.
2 Some individual sounds poorly articulated so that comprehension is sometimes difficult.
1 Individual sounds so poor that comprehension is often impossible.
0 Unintelligible judged on individual sounds.

5 Interactive communication

5 Wholly effective at communicating both actively and receptively in all contexts.
4 Communicates effectively and with ease in most contexts, experiencing only occasional difficulty.
3 Communicates with ease in everyday contexts and adequately in more abstract contexts.
2 Communication effective in everyday contexts but needing patience in more abstract contexts.
1 Communicates poorly even in everyday contexts.
0 Communicates nothing.

6 Vocabulary resource

5 Wide-ranging, varied, precise and appropriate in all contexts.
4 Shows few vocabulary gaps other than in specialised areas. Rarely needs to paraphrase.
3 Adequate on general tasks, though sometimes needs to resort to paraphrase.
2 Vocabulary though adequate for everyday tasks seldom rises above the mundane.
1 Lack of vocabulary makes performance even in everyday contexts inadequate.
0 Vocabulary too slight for communication at this level.

After each interview, listen to the examiners discussing the marks.

HINTS FOR SUCCESS

Here are some tips to remember when you sit the Proficiency exam.

GENERAL
Always read the instructions carefully. Most of the standard instructions are shown in the practice tests in this book, so make sure you look at them carefully. But there may be some small variations in the exam itself, so be prepared.

Make sure you know how long each paper lasts. Before you go into the exam, it is a good idea to decide how much time you should spend on each part of the paper.

Paper 1: Reading Comprehension
Remember that the multiple choice questions in the Proficiency exam always have three working answers and one correct one. Don't make the mistake of ticking more than one box! When you read the question, try to decide as soon as possible which answers *are definitely* wrong, then which answers *may be* wrong, then re-read the passage and check. When you do the practice tests, think about why you chose the correct answer and rejected the others.

Always guess; never leave a blank. You never know, you may be lucky!

Always read the passage through once before looking at the questions. It may help you to think of a title for each passage, or a few key words to make sure you read it for its general meaning.

Paper 2: Composition
Make sure you answer the question. You can lose some marks for irrelevance. When you do the practice tests in this book, it is a good idea to look at the composition titles and to think about the possible content of each composition. Make a plan of what to include. Practise this by writing down as many ideas as you can think of in thirty seconds. It's a good idea to make a plan like this in the examination itself. It may take five minutes, but you will write a better composition.

Make sure you don't write too much or too little. If you write too much, you won't have enough time to check. If you write too little, the total mark possible for that composition will be reduced.

Make sure you know how to lay out a letter. It's very important to decide if the composition title demands a formal or an informal letter and to use a suitable layout, phrases and vocabulary.

Paper 3: Use of English
Read the whole passage in the blank-filling exercise before you start answering. Decide what part of speech the missing word is and look carefully at the context. When you've made your choice, read on and check.

Remember that in the blank filling exercise, you can only insert one word. Occasionally, there is more than one possible answer, but you won't get more marks for providing all of them.

Make sure that your sentence in the transformation exercise is as similar as possible in meaning to the sentence which is given on the exam paper. Think about all the changes which you need to make and check that your new sentence is grammatically correct.

Paper 4: Listening Comprehension
Look at the answer paper very quickly to get an idea of what the listening passage is likely to be about. Each time you do a practice paper from this book, try to predict the possible content of the passage before you begin listening. Think about the situation, the number of people and their roles as well.

Answer the obvious questions first. Use the pause between the two playbacks of the passage to check these answers, and to eliminate any choices which are obviously wrong for the remaining questions. During the second playback, concentrate on the remaining questions. Don't leave any questions without an answer; if necessary, make a guess.

Paper 5: Interview
Practise a few phrases which you can say if you need time to think.
Make a list of phrases like; *I'm sorry, I didn't hear (you) . . . I don't quite understand what you're getting at . . . Could you repeat the question, please?* which you can use when the examiner asks a difficult question.

Don't try to read and understand every word of documents which the examiner may give you in the last part of the interview. Often, authentic material is used and it may consist of a lot of text. But the examiner won't ask you detailed questions about it, just about its general idea.

Keep calm! Easier said than done, but the examiner will do his/her best to help you relax, as this is the best way to find out how well you speak English.

Simon Greenall

TEST ONE

PAPER 1 READING COMPREHENSION 1 hour

SECTION A

In this section you must choose the word or phrase which best completes each sentence. **On your answer sheet**, *indicate the letter* **A, B, C** *or* **D** *against the number of each item 1 to 25 for the word or phrase you choose.*

1 It was unfortunate, but she had no _____ but to act as she did.

   A chance   **B** opportunity   **C** option   **D** solution

2 We lost _____ of them in the dense jungle undergrowth.

   A sight   **B** vision   **C** view   **D** vista

3 His recovery after the accident was _____ short of miraculous.

   A not   **B** rather   **C** slightly   **D** little

4 Let's try it another way; it's no _____ doing the same thing again.

   A point   **B** value   **C** good   **D** sense

5 The company might well go to the _____ if business doesn't pick up.

   A floor   **B** wall   **C** ground   **D** street

6 The public have been kept completely in the _____ about the affair.

   A secret   **B** ignorance   **C** dark   **D** darkness

7 I'm really excited; it will be the first time _____ the islands.

   A I've visited   **B** I visit   **C** I'll visit   **D** I'm visiting

8 He's spent a _____ fortune repairing that useless old car.

   A large   **B** little   **C** big   **D** small

9 How did they manage to steal the Van Gogh? It was right _____ the security guard's nose.

   A below   **B** before   **C** under   **D** beside

10 I don't want to worry you, but I think we're _____ low on petrol.

   A going   **B** falling   **C** running   **D** driving

11 She threw a heavy bottle _____ the intruder, but just missed him.

   A at   **B** for   **C** to   **D** towards

12 His work has been very good, but there is still _____ for improvement.

   A space   **B** need   **C** room   **D** hope

13 Although they had signed the peace treaty, they were _____ preparing for a renewed offensive.

   A occupied   **B** busy   **C** engaged   **D** involved

14 While disapproving of their methods, it cannot be _____ that they have made quite a breakthrough.

    A rejected   **B** denied   **C** contradicted   **D** refused

15 He doesn't believe _____ changing his way of life just to suit fashion.

    A that   **B** it   **C** in   **D** on

16 You went dressed like that? It's a _____ they let you in at all!

    A revelation   **B** joke   **C** doubt   **D** wonder

17 The crisis deepened, yet still the government was _____ to act.

    A cautious   **B** opposed   **C** contrary   **D** reluctant

18 I am afraid your passport does not give you the right of _____ in this country.

    A life   **B** stay   **C** living   **D** abode

19 The conversation was _____ by a loud knock at the door.

    A cut out   **B** cut short   **C** cut into   **D** cut through

20 It's the _____ in a series of strikes planned for this, and coming months.

    A ultimate   **B** last   **C** latest   **D** final

21 The verdict was accidental death but the police suspected _____ play.

    A criminal   **B** foul   **C** dirty   **D** murderous

22 The top level talks will be _____ after the weekend break.

    A recovered   **B** reiterated   **C** restated   **D** resumed

23 She takes _____ in spoiling things for everyone else.

    A enjoyment   **B** pleasure   **C** fun   **D** delight

24 Alcohol on an empty stomach _____ my head very quickly.

    A goes round   **B** goes into   **C** goes to   **D** goes through

25 I'm sorry, but walking all the way doesn't _____ to me one bit.

    A appeal   **B** tempt   **C** apply   **D** seem

SECTION B

In this section you will find after each of the passages a number of questions or unfinished statements about the passage, each with four suggested answers or ways of finishing. You must choose the one which you think fits best according to the passage. **On your answer sheet**, *indicate the letter* **A, B, C,** *or* **D** *against the number of each item* **26** *to* **40** *for the answer you choose. Give* **one answer only** *to each question. Read each passage right through before choosing your answers.*

FIRST PASSAGE

'The weekend began at 8 am on Friday. By 3 pm on Sunday I'd had an hour's sleep. I was shaking with exhaustion and I felt too sick to eat. I was about to lie down when my phone went again. I had to admit someone, which stopped me getting any sleep at all. That took me through to Monday, when I would fall asleep whenever I sat down. I felt like crying because I couldn't concentrate. I'd try to write down a clerking and I couldn't remember what I'd asked. All I could think of was another eight hours, another seven hours, another six hours. . . .'

Liz's story is part of the pattern of life as a junior doctor. She works a one-in-three rota, which means that, in addition to working from 8.30 am to 6.30 pm every weekday, she works every third night and every third weekend. Nights off are spent trying to catch up on sleep. Another doctor recalls working 126 hours a week during her first house job. At one point she worked 26 days with only eight nights and not a single day off.

No pilot would be allowed to fly an aeroplane having worked 80 hours on the trot, but if you come into hospital for an operation on a Monday, you might well be operated on by a junior doctor who has been working non-stop since Friday morning. A recent report from the Policy Studies Institute found that 46 per cent of doctors who qualified in 1981 wish they had never entered medicine, compared with 16 per cent in 1966.

Jo is one of the 46 per cent. She gave up medicine because she felt that, working 88 hours a week, she could not do the job to her own satisfaction. One Tuesday night on-call, after a weekend on-call, she nearly gave a child an adult's dose of a strong painkiller. An alert nurse spotted the mistake. Jo lost almost a stone in weight over a few months. She would get home too tired to eat. She also had a chest infection, but did not take time off (although she could have passed the infection on to patients, with serious consequences).

Doctors are among the most likely members of society to become divorced or alcoholic. Their suicide rate is three times the national average.

26 From Friday morning until Monday, Liz

    A did not sleep at all.
    B slept once.
    C slept twice.
    D slept several times.

27 In four weeks Liz would work

    A   3 nights.
    B   6 nights.
    C   9 nights.
    D 12 nights.

28 The comparison with pilots suggests that doctors

    A have less responsibility for people's lives.
    B should have their hours of work controlled.
    C are more competent, even when tired.
    D refuse to have their hours of work controlled.

29 Jo thinks that

    A she should not have become a doctor.
    B she is overworked at the hospital.
    C medicine is not a satisfying profession.
    D what happened to the child was her fault.

30 Both Liz and Jo

    A missed a meal on one occasion.
    B became considerably thinner.
    C found concentration difficult when tired.
    D were physically ill.

SECOND PASSAGE

Whenever I travel I see the same person. Since I am uncertain whether he is a projection of my own mind or whether he has an objective existence, I should be interested to know whether other people have seen him as well.

He is easily described. He stands about 5ft 10in and is in his early or mid-forties. His face is of handsome proportions, tanned with no beard or moustache, and he has fairly short, slightly greying hair. He is dressed in bleached or stone-washed denim jacket and trousers (they are not exactly jeans) and on his feet he wears what were once called 'pumps', then 'sneakers', and now 'trainers'.

Among the characteristics of this man are that he appears to travel alone, carries an air of total but unassuming self-assurance, and is on familiar though businesslike terms with every hotel receptionist, airline clerk or bartender with whom he is speaking. But the most distinguishing thing of all about him is that the only thing he can be imagined as doing is to be on holiday. I have seen him only in airport hotels, in departure lounges, or at baggage reclaim on return, so that I cannot say for certain where he spends his time. I am certain, however, that he goes to Southern Europe and the Caribbean – though come to think of it when I last saw him about a month ago he was about to board a ferry across the Baltic.

Another puzzling thing about this man is that he doesn't look especially wealthy, yet it is impossible to imagine him behind a desk, at a work-bench, or on a tractor. Possibly he is a spy. Possibly he is a policeman tracking drug smugglers. I don't have the impression, though, that he does any work at all. He roams the world like the Flying Dutchman or the Duke of Windsor, except that he doesn't find the travel irksome as they did. I conclude that he was made redundant on generous terms some years ago. If it weren't for the stone-washed denims he might go unobserved, but it is they, which are not quite the gear for a man of his age, that attract attention and give him, such is his omnipresence at every point of departure, a somewhat sinister appearance.

31 The writer knows

  A that the man really exists.
  B what the man looks like.
  C that the man exists only in his imagination.
  D that many readers know what the man looks like.

32 What is noticeable about the way the man dresses?

  A He wears a variety of different kinds of shoes.
  B He is a little too old for the clothes he wears.
  C He is never seen in casual clothes.
  D He is always expensively dressed.

33 Which of these adjectives could be used to describe the man's personality?

  A Conceited.
  B Lonely.
  C Nervous.
  D Confident.

34 The man always seems to be travelling

  A by air.
  B for pleasure.
  C without suitcases.
  D on business.

35 The writer thinks that the man

  A lost his job.
  B is an aristocrat.
  C is employed by a government department.
  D inherited a lot of money.

THIRD PASSAGE

Sick Building Syndrome (SBS) is reported by almost all westernised countries, and is associated with but not confined to air-conditioned office buildings. The phenomenon is defined by its symptoms rather than its cause, since, despite considerable international research, the cause remains unknown. Sufferers experience a range of minor ailments such as headache, dry throat, stuffy nose and irritated eyes, and typically find relief on leaving their workplace.

Research to date has confirmed that the condition is genuine, although there has been and still is great scepticism, possibly because it had tended to be people in lower-grade jobs, and women more than men, who have complained of it. The condescending attitude among doubters that these people 'imagine' symptoms for which there is no identifiable cause, ignores the fact that it is often they who work under the meanest conditions, with the cheapest furniture, with least space and least personal control over their immediate environment.

Press reports have tended further to obscure the issue by confusing sick building syndrome with outbreaks of sickness within buildings such as legionnaires' disease, caused by bacteria, and with such unrelated phenomena as fumes from furniture and carpeting.

These problems are real enough, but they are not SBS. Some interesting correlations have, however, shown up during investigations. For instance, a recent Danish study into SBS, comparing rate of incidence between civic buildings, uncovered a distinct parallel between the surface volume of soft furnishing (rather unpleasantly termed 'fleece') and reports of SBS. As yet the reason is unclear, but an assumption has been made that dust and other fine debris easily harboured within a fibrous surface are to blame, possibly because such material fosters micro-organisms.

A view that static electricity generated by soft furnishings contributes to the syndrome is not supported by research so far, but in Denmark and Italy they are sufficiently persuaded by it to have made efforts to reduce 'fleeceage'.

There are other hypotheses. Sheena Wilson, co-author of the *Office Environment Survey*, published last year by consultants to the building industry, Building Use Studies, believes stress-related factors may also be at work, and that SBS is likely to be multi-causal.

'Badly planned offices often reflect a poor general standard of management which runs through the company, unsettling employees. Standards of maintenance and cleanliness may be poor in such a firm, with little attention paid to adequate lighting, space, comfort and so on.'

The effect, she argues, is not only physical. A lack of any proper system of building management communicates itself to the workers. They sense and see the chaos, the absence of care, and feel that their needs are disregarded.

Wilson recommends various remedies, including overhaul and maintenance of ventilation systems, attention to lighting (with furnishings chosen to enhance available natural light), and regular, thorough cleaning routines.

36 Those studying SBS

   A now know why it happens but are only looking at the symptoms.

   B know what the symptoms are but have not determined the reasons for it.

   C know it is due to air-conditioning but have not established why.

   D have not found out why it only occurs in the western hemisphere.

37 According to the writer, scepticism about SBS is

   A commonsense.

   B insane.

   C scientifically-based.

   D arrogant.

38 Research has shown that 'fumes from furniture and carpeting'

   A may exist where there is SBS.

   B are an invention of the media.

   C can lead to legionnaires' disease.

   D are caused by micro-organisms.

39 In Denmark and Italy

   A nobody believes that soft furnishings are to blame.

   B moves to reduce soft furnishing are foreseen.

   C static electricity is regarded as the cause.

   D there have already been moves to reduce soft furnishing.

40 Sheena Wilson says that SBS could be due to

   A unscrupulous employers who refuse to improve working conditions.

   B unpleasant conditions and the resulting staff alienation.

   C workers feeling that the company does not care about them.

   D dark, dirty, cramped, uncomfortable and poorly-ventilated offices.

PAPER 2 COMPOSITION 2 hours

*Write **two only** of the following composition exercises. Your answers must follow exactly the instructions given. Write in pen, not pencil. You are allowed to make alterations, but make sure you work is clear and easy to read.*

1   Describe a TV commercial which has caught the public imagination in your country. (About 350 words)

2   'Religious intolerance is on the increase.' Discuss. (About 350 words)

3   Tell the story of a stay in the worst hotel imaginable. (About 350 words)

4   Write a letter in reply to the following: (About 300 words)

> We have been instructed to place this announcement by our client, a wealthy retired industrialist. He is prepared to make a gift of ten million dollars to the person, of any nationality, who can convince him that this sum would be spent in the most constructive way possible. Send proposals, which should be amiable but down-to-earth in tone, to: "Philanthropist", P.O. Box 73595.

5   Set books.

PAPER 3   USE OF ENGLISH   2 hours

SECTION A

1   *Fill each of the numbered blanks in the passage with **one** suitable word.*

The gruelling assault course can have punishing physical and _____(1) effects which _____(2) to be unpredictable from one individual _____(3) another. Dehydration _____(4) shedding pints of perspiration in marching, crawling and climbing _____ (5) a series of high walls in full kit can _____(6) to almost complete disorientation _____(7) some young men. One large muscular youth had to be helped _____(8) from a route march between two of his mates, one supporting him under _____(9) arm. He was taken before the NCOs, working from a concrete blockhouse in the exercise yard, and asked what was _____(10) with him. He produced _____(11) reply, looking dumbly _____(12) ahead _____(13) if in _____(14) world.

A hot cup of tea with plenty of reviving sugar in it practically had to be forced _____(15) his mouth because he would not or could not push his head two inches _____(16) to take a drink from the proferred cup. He was finally sent back to camp in a truck for medical _____ (17), and subsequently disappeared from the Marines.

On the other _____(18), the flow of adrenalin can produce remarkable results. Recruits can be almost oblivious _____(19) bleeding hands, elbows and faces as they crawl over rough terrain, and only become _____(20) of them when they are back in camp.

---

2   *Finish each of the following sentences in such a way that it is as similar as possible in meaning to the sentence printed before it.*

Example: He talks a lot more than his sister.
Answer: He's *a lot more talkative than his sister.*

a   What's the point of going to the meeting?

Is _____

b   Despite his brilliance, he never became famous.

Brilliant _____

c   You won't see cliffs like these anywhere else in the world.

Nowhere _____

d   Even if it takes all day the job's got to be finished.

However _____

e The reasons for the delay are not yet clear.

It is not yet clear _____

f He didn't know what to do next so he rang me up.

Not _____

g All the crew members were killed in the explosion.

Not a _____

h The car wouldn't start, which annoyed him intensely.

To his _____

3   *Fill each of the blanks with a suitable word or phrase.*

Example: Half the young people round here are ____*on the*____ dole

a They look identical! How can you _____ is which?

b It won't be long _____ fed up with that job.

c Should _____ any help, just call me.

d Has it ever _____ that you might be wasting your time?

e We had a lovely holiday, but on _____ we found the house had been burgled.

f It really is time he retired. By June he _____ working there for 40 years.

4   *For each of the sentences below, write a new sentence as similar as possible in meaning to the original sentence, but using the word given. This word **must not be altered** in any way.*

Example: You've really upset her.
        feelings
Answer: *You've really hurt her feelings.*

a I have no intention of paying him.
prepared

_____

b He got to the meeting two minutes before it was due to begin.
spare

_____

c We are not entirely happy about your plans.
misgivings

_____

d Would you like me to drive you to the airport?
lift

_____

e He spends all day sleeping.
but

_____

f   When the sun went down, the temperature fell sharply.
fall

_____

g   Demonstrations outside the palace are not permitted.
ban

_____

h   The Minister has authorised the project.
go-ahead

_____

SECTION B

5   *Read the following passage, then answer the questions which follow it.*

Frankly, I was not enjoying the journey. We were halfway up the Karakoram Highway (KKH), a
long slash in a perpendicular lunar landscape of gigantic proportions forming the world's most
fearsome major road. Halted at a police roadblock, we could hear two feuding sects firing shots
across the chasm ahead of us.

Boulders had been levered on to our path from the great brown scree above, so we turned back to   5
the one-street village of Komila to find a teahouse until the all-clear signal came. My guide Rayaz,
his brother Vager and our driver Azad ordered samosas and green tea while I strolled out of earshot
to rehearse a vital discovery in my Urdu phrasebook: *Ahista chalaiye gari* – drive slowly.

For many of its 500 miles the KKH teeters precariously above the sinuous grey torrents of the
Indus River. Safety barriers are rare and rockfalls, wandering goats and lunatic oncoming truck   10
drivers frequent. Azad, a tall and ever-smiling Stevie Wonder lookalike with permanent dark
glasses, was intent on getting us to our destination in the far North of Pakistan in time for supper.
Thus the musical chimes emitted from the dashboard of our dusty white Corolla whenever we
exceeded 100kph rang intermittently throughout the dazzling day.

The fighting herdsmen were dispersed after a couple of hours and we moved on, under jeep escort   15
at first, to Gilgit. The scenery became more exaggerated around every hairpin as the stony highway
skewered and roller-coasted to the point at which three of the world's highest mountain ranges –
the Himalayas, Karakorams and Hindu Kush – slam into each other. Azad, his accelerator foot now
about an inch higher, reached the hotel long after dark. The chef had given us up and gone home
and I accepted the blame for a meagre meal of plain omelettes produced by a sympathetic porter.   20

The Pakistanis bill the KKH as 'a 20th-century miracle', opening only in 1978 after 11 years' work
and the deaths of 3000 labourers. It follows the line of the historic silk route from China to the sub-
continent. Until its completion, travel in the region was mainly by camel and pony.

The reasons for driving a motor road through such hostile terrain are debatable. The truck
caravans between Pakistan and China roll just once a year, while the northern tribesmen and their   25
families continue to live at subsistence level in a manner unchanged by centuries.

The road crept along the side of intimidating cliffs, the boiling river far below. Stunning views of
Rakaposhi, a 25,551ft shimmering pinnacle of ice and rock, were a dangerous distraction. Suddenly
the gorge opened out into a fertile valley walled with terraces of maize and millet and orchards of
apricots and peaches. Past the Hunza ruby mine, we turned up the mountainside and along poplar   30
and plane lined dirt tracks to a village, Karimabad, that must remain indelible on any memory. Here,
if it exists at all (although an inn farther back on the KKH claimed the name) was Shangri-la.

The Hunzakuts are the friendliest of people, and their apparent longevity due to gold in the water
is legendary. Perversely we ordered Coca Colas at a new rest house and started back for the Punjab
plains where the KKH slides through rice paddies and sugar cane fields and the potent aroma of wild   35
marijuana rises from the roadsides.

After a rush-hour tour of Lahore I was convinced of Azad's driving brilliance. At the airport I
gave him a tip of 200 rupees and indicated that he should buy himself some new dark glasses,
since one lens was badly cracked – a defect which had added to my concern on the KKH. He lifted
off his shades for the first time to reveal one smiling eye and one badly bloodshot. He grinned and   40
held up a solitary finger. 'Only one eye?' I asked. He nodded.

a Why is the Karakoram Highway descibed as 'a long slash' (line 2)?

_____

b Explain in your own words what was happening while the writer was at the police roadblock.

_____

c What did the author do when the others were in the teahouse?

_____

d What was the purpose of the 'musical chimes' (line 13)?

_____

e What is meant by a 'hairpin', as it is used on line 16?

_____

f Give another expression for 'slam into each other' (line 18).

_____

g Why did the author accept the blame for the 'meagre meal'?

_____

h Why does the author use the word 'bill' on line 21?

_____

i Why was the KKH built?

_____

j Why is the author sceptical about its usefulness?

_____

k What is meant by 'the boiling river' on line 27?

_____

l Explain the phrase 'poplar and plane lined dirt tracks' (lines 30–31)

_____

m What was perverse about ordering 'Coca Colas at a new rest house' (line 34)?

_____

n How important was the 'defect' on line 39 and what were the author's feelings about it during the drive?

_____

_____

o   In a paragraph of 70–90 words, summarise the dangers faced by the author on the KKH.

_____

_____

_____

_____

_____

_____

_____

_____

_____

_____

_____

PAPER 4 LISTENING COMPREHENSION about 30 minutes

FIRST PART

For questions 1–6 put a tick in one of the boxes A, B, C or D.

1 Which of these did **not** take place in the performance of *4 minutes 33 seconds?*

   A Somebody walked onto the stage.

   B He sat down at a piano.

   C He played the piano.

   D He walked off the stage.

A	
B	
C	
D	

2 What was the content of *4 minutes 33 seconds?*

   A Nothing

   B Noises made by people watching the pianist

   C Performers following written instructions

   D Musicians greeting one another

A	
B	
C	
D	

3 The 1960s minimalists

   A rejected the values of the rich and powerful.

   B were apolitical.

   C wanted a bigger share of the profits from their work.

   D at first concentrated mainly on literature.

A	
B	
C	
D	

4 Why would they regard *Equivalent 8* as a failure?

   A It has been ignored by the critics.

   B It is not worth as much as other works of art.

   C Most people laughed at it.

   D It now has a high market value.

A	
B	
C	
D	

5 Bedford says that minimalist composers

   A write better music for instruments than for singers.

   B are far too conservative.

   C write better melodies than Mozart, Wagner or Brahms.

   D have never written anything innovative.

A	
B	
C	
D	

6 According to Kenyon minimalist music has a future as a creative force because

   A more people are listening to it.

   B it is no longer obsessed with purity and clarity.

   C there will never be such a thing as a minimalist opera.

   D it can easily be distinguished from other kinds of music.

A	
B	
C	
D	

SECOND PART

For questions 7–10 put a tick in one of the boxes A, B, C or D.

7 Which drawing shows the position of the handle?

A   B   C   D

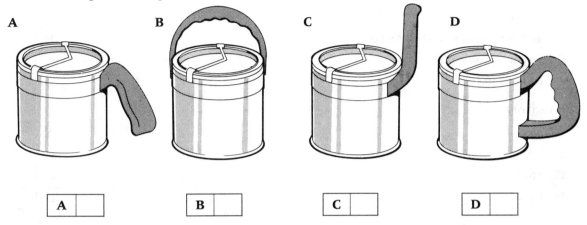

A		B		C		D	

8 Other features include

A   a variety of colour combinations.

B   an adjustable ring attached to the handle.

C   a set of rings for different-sized tins.

D   a range of handle sizes.

A	
B	
C	
D	

9 The purpose of the v-clip is to prevent paint from

A   getting onto surfaces that have already been painted.

B   dripping back into the can.

C   smearing the person using the brush.

D   drying out if the painter is interrupted.

A	
B	
C	
D	

10 Who will probably use the can-holder?

A   decorators

B   artists

C   soldiers

D   telephonists

A	
B	
C	
D	

THIRD PART

For questions 11–16 tick one of the boxes A, B, C or D.

11 Which of these are used in English to mean *overcome difficulties*?

    A To pull the chestnuts out of the fire

    B To take the snake out of the hole

    C To get the cow off the ice

    D None of them

A	
B	
C	
D	

12 Which of these can always be translated?

    A ideas

    B jokes

    C proverbs

    D poetry

A	
B	
C	
D	

13 According to the interpreters, speakers at conferences

    A try to confuse the interpreters.

    B do not care about the problems they cause for interpreters.

    C never write their own speeches.

    D sometimes forget where they have put their false teeth.

A	
B	
C	
D	

14 The speakers that most annoy interpreters

    A talk complete nonsense.

    B do not read their speeches in advance.

    C are mentally unbalanced.

    D deny they said something.

A	
B	
C	
D	

15 *Why couldn't we have made a better job of it?*
The tone of this remark implies

    A anger.

    B regret.

    C perplexity.

    D sarcasm.

A	
B	
C	
D	

16 Throughout the discussion, the male interpreter seems

    A embittered.

    B elated.

    C resigned.

    D calm.

A	
B	
C	
D	

FOURTH PART

For questions 17 and 18 fill in the Tokyo rates, and for question 19 tick the appropriate boxes for the London rates.

TOKYO (closing US Dollar rates)

17 Japanese Yen _____

18 Pound Sterling _____

LONDON (latest currency rates)

19

		rise	fall
a	Pound Sterling		
b	German Mark		
c	Japanese Yen		
d	Australian Dollar		

PAPER 5 INTERVIEW

The theme of this Test is **Traffic**.

1 a Look at *one* of the photographs and describe:
  ☐ the setting,
  ☐ objects of interest,
  ☐ how the driver(s) probably feel(s).

  b Now discuss:
  ☐ solutions to urban traffic problems,
  ☐ how to improve road safety,
  ☐ the psychology of driving.

2   Study *one* of these passages. You may quote from it if you wish.

a   The Campaign for Lead-free Air is probably supported by anti-capitalists. We can see only three reasons for the anti-lead movement; support by precious metal producers who want the catalytic converters; support by engineering groups who believe they will have new facilities to install; or support by leftist-sponsored, anti-big-business groups. We think the third is most likely.

b   The skill of driving in the capital is to keep the element of surprise on your side. Weave from lane to lane, or – better still – straddle them. This is a town where, since no one stops when the lights change to amber, there is a good chance that the car behind you will go straight into the back if you do so yourself. Many of the motorists clearly believe that zebra crossings are for better identifying targets. Pedestrians prefer to avoid them.

c   Anyone who has ever wondered why the interior rear-view mirror often seems to need adjusting for the drive home after work need not blame the car. Apparently, we all shrink three-quarters of an inch during the day as gravity compresses our spines.

Where do you think the text is taken from?
Who do you think the speaker or writer might be?
What is the purpose of the text?
Discuss the content.

3   Do *one* of these tasks.

a   You and your friend(s) are going abroad on holiday by car.
What preparations will you have to make? Discuss the following:
☐   the car
☐   the necessary documents
☐   the route
☐   what to take with you
☐   where all the luggage will go

b   Prepare a short talk on one of these topics:
☐   alternative forms of transport
☐   the ideal car or motorbike
☐   the attraction of speed

TEST TWO

PAPER 1 READING COMPREHENSION 1 hour

SECTION A

In this section you must choose the word or phrase which best completes each sentence. **On your answer sheet**, *indicate the letter* **A, B, C** *or* **D** *against the number of each item 1 to 25 for the word or phrase you choose.*

1 After hours of argument we finally _____ a compromise.

    A reached   **B** came   **C** arrived   **D** had

2 Everything is under control and there is absolutely no cause for _____ .

    A worry   **B** concern   **C** dread   **D** panic

3 I know everyone here is confident, but there are _____ who say we'll lose.

    A these   **B** they   **C** those   **D** them

4 There'll be noise, fumes and congestion, not to _____ the destruction of a listed building.

    A mention   **B** say   **C** comment   **D** remark

5 There are some very attractive properties _____ offer round here.

    A in   **B** for   **C** on   **D** at

6 There were mutual accusations, but in the _____ analysis he was to blame.

    A recent   **B** overall   **C** objective   **D** final

7 Despite her apparent sincerity, no-one was _____ by her explanation.

    A taken over   **B** taken in   **C** taken aback   **D** taken off

8 Six straight victories mean they are a team to be _____ with.

    A reckoned   **B** beaten   **C** calculated   **D** won

9 It's a great opportunity; try and _____ the most of it.

    A do   **B** have   **C** make   **D** take

10 I really do object _____ the television on all the time.

    A having   **B** to have   **C** to having   **D** to have had

11 All that effort; and now he's got nothing to _____ for it.

    A show   **B** demonstrate   **C** work   **D** spend

12 Ensure there is at least a 3cm space _____ allow adequate ventilation.

    A by so doing   **B** so that   **C** in doing so   **D** so as to

13 Why ask me? _____ all I know she might be living abroad by now.

    A Though   **B** Since   **C** For   **D** Despite

14 If they're looking for trouble when we get outside, just stay _____ .

    A cold   **B** tepid   **C** cool   **D** icy

15 _____ being the coldest winter on record, it's also been the wettest.

    A Moreover   **B** Besides   **C** Beside   **D** Furthermore

16 Let's not forget there are other factors to be _____ into consideration.

    A looked   **B** put   **C** mentioned   **D** taken

17 It's after eleven so we _____ better be making a move.

    A had   **B** would   **C** should   **D** are

18 _____ a good time when you stay with them?

    A Have you   **B** Do you have   **C** Are you having   **D** Have you got

19 I've played bridge, but poker is by far my favourite _____ .

    A sport   **B** hobby   **C** game   **D** diversion

20 The patient is _____ a series of tests to determine the actual cause.

    A undergoing   **B** experiencing   **C** experimenting   **D** suffering

21 Following the well-publicised scandal, the President has been asked to _____ .

    A step up   **B** step into   **C** step down   **D** step over

22 It's time you started thinking about _____ your own living.

    A working   **B** employing   **C** gaining   **D** earning

23 You did not have _____ permission to take the day off.

    A the   **B** my   **C** some   **D** a

24 After several delays, they _____ launch the space shuttle last night.

    A could   **B** might   **C** were able to   **D** had the possibility to

25 For the best visual effect, sit directly _____ the screen.

    A against   **B** opposite   **C** in view of   **D** opposite to

SECTION B

*In this section you will find after each of the passages a number of questions or unfinished statements about the passage, each with four suggested answers or ways of finishing. You must choose the one which you think fits best according to the passage. **On your answer sheet**, indicate the letter **A, B, C** or **D** against the number of each item **26** to **40** for the answer you choose. Give **one answer only** to each question. Read each passage right through before choosing your answers.*

FIRST PASSAGE

Technical language, in craft and science, exists for two purposes. One is to allow specialists to talk with ease about things for which common parlance has no terms. The other is to bamboozle the uninitiated into thinking there's more to the subject than there really is. What professional body does not use this technique to impress upon the government and the public how essential their mysterious abilities are? What hapless academics do not cram the latest buzzwords into their dead-duck research proposals in a (not always) vain attempt to breathe a semblance of life into grant applications? What, after all, are scientists but professional men and women who, in the words of John Galloway (*New Scientist*, February 28, p43) are merely 'trying to get on'? The mystique of science serves some very important ends which it may not be in their interests to dispel.

As convenor of a conference, I once had a 150-word abstract sent to me. Despite being myself a specialist in the subject, I was unable to understand anything of the paper being described. Yet the sentences were correctly constructed, and gave a semblance of logic. The problem was vocab.

I wrestled with it for a whole day. Eventually, by combing references on related topics in American journals, and by examining some outdated glossaries, I worked out the main thrust of the implications in this great work. If I mentioned them by name, perhaps a non-palaeontologist would not see the sense of it. But the contention turned out to be no more complex (and not a lot more significant) than 'some oranges have pips'. Not an unimportant observation, perhaps, but hardly a world-shattering piece of news. Put like that, indeed, a little short on mystique. But then, great thoughts, simply expressed, do have the beauty of simplicity.

26 Technical language enables those who use it
to

   A avoid slang and vulgar expressions
   B explain complicated ideas to ordinary
      people with more precision.
   C pretend their speciality is too complex
      for others to understand.
   D show the public how sophisticated their
      speciality is.

27 What is the significance of '(not always)'?

   A Academics are sometimes quite modest.
   B They may not want their proposals to be
      accepted.
   C Obtaining a grant might not be their real
      aim.
   D Their use of jargon is sometimes
      successful.

28 The writer of the text suggests that scientists

   A want to improve relations with the
      opposite sex.
   B might benefit from using obscure
      language.
   C expect to be understood by non-
      specialists.
   D have not been taught how to write
      properly.

29 After studying the abstract, the writer

   A at last understood the details.
   B was still not sure whether he had got the
      gist of it or not.
   C finally realised it in fact said nothing at
      all.
   D got the general idea in the end.

30 The writer of the text is

   A a craftsman.
   B a scientist.
   C a language expert.
   D a politician.

SECOND PASSAGE

Laser printers, combined with personal computers and document-generating software, are part of that growing phenomenon, desk-top publishing, known as DTP. Today such systems allow anyone to produce almost typeset-quality manuscripts. Where early printers left quite a lot to be desired, the latest inexpensive ones are very impressive. As with a good video recorder, it is possible to tell that the output isn't 'real', but casual glancers will be fooled.

Within an hour of unpacking a new printer in the office, we'd persuaded it to generate a page of our documentation laid out and typeset in the same way as IBM's technical references. Not just close – the characters, tables, graphics and page numbering were spot-on. Fancy that, we thought. And most users will probably leave it there, content to use the new technology as the makers intend.

But like most innovative products, there are uncharted byways where the over-creative can over-indulge. Most office workers will have experienced mock memos which, ranging from the obviously fake to the subtly mischievous, inform the workforce of new unisex toilets or the company electric chair scheme.

These are common because all the bits needed to make them up – corporate letterhead, typewriter and photocopier – are readily to hand. A good DTP system with a laser printer offers the prankster much more: the equivalent of a design studio and professional printing press in two small boxes.

For starters, take the unloved but perennially popular Metropolitan Police parking ticket. For some time these have been officially produced with a laser printer on plain white paper – which makes them the ideal first-time target for a joker. In one lunchtime, he (it's usually a he) could produce enough dodgy parking tickets to panic a boardroom full of Porsche owners.

False disc labels, misleading pages for ring-bound manuals, or even completely concocted instruction leaflets are all tempting targets for the office fool with a warped sense of humour and a mouse.

A friend has produced a lapel badge identifying him as a prominent member of a major European research organisation that doesn't quite exist. But it looks the part. If enough people were to turn up at an establishment wearing such insignia, it would need a very brave doorman to turn them away. All it takes to produce cartloads of this sort of thing is an eye for current corporate style and a desktop publishing system.

There are even more devious and culpable uses for DTP. Buying departments the world over know of the telex directory fraud. An enterprising fellow got a load of fake invoices printed up at considerable expense, purporting to be bills for inclusion in an international telex listing. He mailed these to a selection of large companies, most of whose overworked secretaries sent a cheque by return. With access to an office laser printer, the 'considerable expense' aspect of cons like that goes away, and almost anyone can play.

31 The early printers

   A could not produce high-quality manuscripts.
   B were unpopular in some offices.
   C tended to leave gaps on the pages.
   D made people wish they could afford them.

32 When the writer and his colleagues saw how good the printer was, they

   A wanted one each.
   B were surprised.
   C thought someone had played a trick on them.
   D began to think of tricks to play on other people.

33 DTP in the office may lead to.

   A the majority of staff misusing the system.
   B some people finding new ways of misusing the system.
   C staff producing far too much material.
   D changes in the facilities for office workers.

34 DTP enables anyone to

   A forge documents.
   B pose as a policeman.
   C take control of companies.
   D type efficiently.

35 The false lapel badge

   A could be worn with a fashionable business suit.
   B did not fool the doorman.
   C is a near-perfect imitation of the original.
   D should give the wearer certain privileges.

36 The story of the telex directory fraud is included to show

   A the new spirit of individual initiative in present-day society.
   B the potential for crime using desk-top publishing.
   C the incompetence of secretaries everywhere.
   D that DTP can be a source of inexpensive amusement.

THIRD PASSAGE

Extract 1

What can a snorer do to minimise the problem? Inventors have patented commercial versions of old folk remedies, such as the 'snore ball' – something hard fixed to the back to deter the snorer from lying on his or her back. Other gadgets include mouth gags, muzzles, chin-straps and special collars 'to stop the neck kinking'. These methods may help those who snore mildly and do not suffer from OSA (obstructive sleep apnoea – the word apnoea comes from the Greek for 'without breath'), but they are fairly useless and may be dangerous if used by people who are more seriously affected, particularly if their nose is already blocked.

Extract 2

People with apnoea seem more likely to report disturbed sleep, and to put this down to insomnia. Their doctors then prescribe them various sleeping pills or tranquillisers, since anxiety is the usual cause of poor sleep. But anxiety is not the cause in this case, and while these drugs do not cause OSA, they can further depress the respiratory drive. More importantly, however, because their function is to promote sleep, they make it more difficult for the individual to respond to the emergency signals to wake up. They thus usually prolong the apnoeic episodes, causing the level of oxygen in the blood to fall further.

Extract 3

The most promising treatment to date, pioneered by a leading Australian investigator, Colin Sullivan, of the University of Sydney, is called 'nasal airway positive pressure'. Throughout sleep, the patient wears a fitted nose mask coupled to a pump supplying air at slightly above atmospheric pressure. Provided that no air leaks out around the mask, the higher air pressure keeps the oropharynx from collapsing. The device can easily be used at home, though the sight of someone wearing it is rather offputting. The method is harmless, seems to be extremely effective, and often eliminates OSA.

Extract 4

Johnson's solution uses music as the antidote. His device comprises an automatic tape recorder complete with cassette of the snorer's favourite music. A pad under the pillow containing a miniature speaker and a special microphone on the bedside table are both connected to the tape recorder. The microphone picks up the sound of snoring and activates the tape which begins playing very softly – so as not to disturb the snorer's partner. It increases in volume very gently and stops as soon as the microphone ceases to pick up snoring, when the culprit has been gently wakened. It starts again as soon as the snoring resumes.

37 Which extract refers to a faulty diagnosis?

   A Extract 1
   B Extract 2
   C Extract 3
   D Extract 4

38 In which extract does the writer consider the treatment slightly ridiculous?

   A Extract 1
   B Extract 2
   C Extract 3
   D Extract 4

39 In which of these extracts is a treatment described which might be dangerous for OSA sufferers?

   A Extract 1
   B Extract 2
   C Extracts 1 and 2
   D Neither extract 1 nor extract 2

40 In which of these extracts is a treatment described which might bother people who live with the snorer?

   A Extract 3
   B Extract 4
   C Extracts 3 and 4
   D Neither extract 3 nor extract 4

PAPER 2 COMPOSITION 2 hours

*Write **two only** of the following composition exercises. Your answers must follow exactly the instructions given. Write in pen, not pencil. You are allowed to make alterations, but make sure your work is clear and easy to read.*

1 Describe the laziest person you know. (About 350 words)

2 Describe aspects of society which you feel have got better or worse since you were a child. (About 350 words)

3 Write about an event which changed the course of your country's recent history. (About 350 words)

4 After a long journey by air you find out your luggage has been lost. Using the ticket and picture prompts below to help you, write to the airline telling them:
☐ the flight details
☐ at what stage of the journey you think the luggage might have been lost
☐ what you did when you realised your cases were missing
☐ what the cases contain
☐ what you expect to be done to find them.
(About 300 words).

ENDORSEMENTS/RESTRICTIONS (CARBON)		ORIGIN/DESTINATION		BOOKING REF		FROM/TO			
NO CHANGES/REFUNDS PERMITTED		CONJUNCTION TICKETS 057 150/3/9/254					CARRIER	FARE CALCULATION	
NAME OF PASSENGER (NOT TRANSFERABLE) JAMIESON A.T. MR		ISSUED IN EXCHANGE FOR		DATE OF ISSUE 5 SEPT	AUDIT COUPON				

NO CHANGES/REFUNDS PERMITTED

JAMIESON A.T. MR

COUPONS NOT VALID BEFORE: 14 MAR 30 APR

COUPONS NOT VALID AFTER: 14 MAR 30 APR

X/O	NOT GOOD FOR PASSAGE	FARE BASIS	ALLOW	CARRIER	FLIGHT	CLASS	DATE	TIME	STATUS
	FROM LONDON (LHR)	YS XIM	20	BA	631	L	14 MAR	12 15	OK
	TO BOMBAY	YS XIM	20	AI	431	L	14 MAR	22 30	OK
	TO KATMANDU	YS XIM	20	AI	432	L	28 APR	23 45	OK
	TO BOMBAY	YS XIM	20	BA	632	L	29 APR	18 30	OK
	TO LONDON (LHR)	GBP	799					COMM 9	TAX

FARE GBP 799

FORM OF PAYMENT AGT/NON REF

PASSENGER TICKET & BAGGAGE CHECK - ISSUED BY

SUBJECT TO CONDITIONS OF CONTRACT IN THE TICKET

GBP 799 EQUIV FARE PD

GBP 799

3923679146 5

5 Set books

PAPER 3 USE OF ENGLISH 2 hours

SECTION A

1 *Fill each of the numbered blanks in the passage with **one** suitable word.*

My own association with the Americans _____(1) back more than 30 years. _____

(2) a young man I had _____(3) enormously enjoyable experience of _____(4) a

year exploring the United States with a travelling fellowship.

My overriding impression _____(5), confirmed in many subsequent visits (two of

_____(6) in the last four months), was _____(7) a huge and disparate country, in

many parts of _____(8) Washington seemed almost as far distant as London. _____

(9) the inhabitants of Idaho or Nebraska, local issues far outweighed _____(10) which

preoccupied the administration two or three thousand miles _____(11) in Washington and

about _____(12) local opinion _____(13) generally both ignorant and unconcerned.

Of course there were and _____(14) exceptions: communities in the heartland

_____(15) the influence _____(16) an exceptionally good newspaper or a

broadminded congressman have _____(17) a closer awareness of the outside _____

(18) and its problems. But these are rare, perhaps _____(19) today than they were

_____(20) the days of Truman or Eisenhower or Kennedy.

2 *Finish each of the following sentences in such a way that it is as similar as possible in meaning to the sentence printed before it.*

Example: Attendance is compulsory.
Answer: It is *compulsory to attend.*

a Why not leave the hardest part till tomorrow?

What's wrong _____?

b In Greece, it's both hot and sunny at this time of the year.

Besides _____

c He refused to obey the order, which was very brave.

It was _____

d What worries them is the initial outlay, rather than the workload.

What worries them is not _____

e A performance of such quality is not often seen anywhere.

Rarely _____

f They constantly encouraged her, which made her job easier.

Their _____

g I found their reaction rather puzzling.

I was _____

h She didn't let them out of her sight for a second.

Not _____

3 *Fill each of the blanks with a suitable word or phrase*

Example: The answer was on ___*the tip of*___ my tongue.

a This is the second time this week that you _____ late.

b You _____ a taxi. The bus came a few seconds later.

c Never in the history of science _____ such a breakthrough.

d I didn't want to go to the party anyway. I'd sooner _____ at home and watched TV.

e I'm sorry for _____ know before, but I couldn't contact you.

f If only _____ my temper with her. We'd still be together now.

4 *For each of the sentences below, write a new sentence as similar as possible in meaning to the original sentence, but using the word given. This word **must not be altered** in any way.*

Example: When did they last get in touch with you?
     hear
Answer: *When did you last hear from them?*

a The aim of this Government has been the elimination of poverty.
sought

_____

b They made him look utterly ridiculous.
fool

_____

c The President did not deny the possibility of further measures.
rule

_____

d I'll talk to him in private
word

_____

e How's the cup final going?
score

_____

f   She's deeply suspicious of anything new.
mistrust

_____

g   We have arranged everything for your stay.
made

_____

h   They were constantly attacked from all directions.
under

_____

SECTION B

5   _Read the following passage, then answer the questions which follow it._

Every week for 20 years two or three pop groups have had new sessions broadcast by John Peel. The list of groups who have bashed out their stuff in the BBC's Maida Vale Studios, a list printed in small type across the _Peel Sessions_ sleeves, reads like a who's who, who will be, and who never-was and never-will-be of pop. With the usual engaging Peel inefficiency, the list features several spelling mistakes and apparently at least one band that never existed.   5

That these cheaply marketed records can succeed is a testament to the allegiance of Peel's fans and the occasional vulnerability of the pop industry to genuine talent. It is also regrettable that the BBC did not help Peel realise his dream sooner.

Peel and his producer John Walters first approached the BBC with the idea of putting the sessions out on record as long ago as the early Seventies, when the artistes being taped included Pink Floyd,   10 the Incredible String Band, Fairport Convention and Family. Nothing happened. In the face of a number of contractual problems, the idea was shelved, until about a year ago.

In the intervening period, groups often paid the BBC to obtain reproduction rights for their sessions, the tracks appearing on or constituting whole LP's. But more common were bootleg recordings, still to be found in record shops across Northern Europe. Last year Peel's patience ran   15 out: it's a bit much when an illegal cassette copy of a session appears openly on sale _the day after_ its first broadcast.

Peel felt the bands were due some money for their work. A year's planning led to the launch of _Strange Fruit Records_ last autumn. The company, run by Clive and Shirley Selwood, exists solely to issue Peel sessions as they were originally recorded and broadcast, with the aim of building up a   20 'truly collectable music archive'. 'But unfortunately, I've just discovered I make no money out of this at all', Peel told the _New Musical Express_ at 'Strange Fruit's' launch party, held in what appeared to be a Radio 1 corridor.

To describe what Strange Fruit has had to do to get the sessions on to vinyl as 'complicated' would be an understatement. First, Peel chooses his favourite sessions. The Selwoods then find out if the   25 tapes still exist. With horrific short-sightedness many sessions from the early days, including what would now be priceless recordings by pop legends, have been wiped by the BBC; and many must simply have been lifted by unscrupulous BBC employees or outsiders. But more and more of the tapes are being found at the back of cupboards all over Broadcasting House.

Next, permission is sought from the artiste's record company. Finally Peel works out the release   30 dates, mainting a balance in much the same way as he chooses music for his programmes, mixing favourites with forgotten classics, new bands with the unusual. The master tapes are obtained from the BBC for a fee and a royalty, 'and then the real work starts', says Clive Selwood. The 16 releases to date have been restricted to the last ten years: sessions from the late Seventies and early Eighties are the most in demand. Listening to these records, one realises why a Peel session can be the perfect   35 record of a group at its best. The producers and engineers at Maida Vale turn out an honest sound, which would not flatter the weak or bland. 'Speaking as a parent', Peel lamented recently, 'it is distressing to see not a single record in the Top 40 of which a parent can disapprove'. There is plenty to disapprove of in these sessions.

a What is meant by 'bashed out their stuff' (line 2)?

_____

_____

b What are the 'never-was and never-will-be of pop' (lines 4–5)?

_____

_____

c In your own words, explain why the records have been a success.

_____

_____

_____

d What happened to Peel's first attempt to issue the sessions on record, and why?

_____

_____

_____

e What was 'the intervening period' referred to on line 13?

_____

_____

f What word or phrase could be used in place of 'bootleg' (line 14)?

_____

_____

g What does 'this' refer to on line 22?

_____

_____

h What is an 'understatement' (line 25)?

_____

_____

i Explain the meaning of 'short-sightedness' as used on line 26.

_____

_____

j   Why do some recordings no longer exist?

_____

_____

k   What are 'release dates' (lines 30–31)?

_____

_____

l   How does Peel ensure balance?

_____

_____

m   What does 'record' mean on line 36?

_____

_____

n   Why is the sound at Maida Vale described as 'honest' (line 36)?

_____

_____

o   In a paragraph of 80–100 words summarise the reasons why *Strange Fruit Records* was set up, and the steps that need to be taken in order to produce a record from the sessions.

_____

_____

_____

_____

_____

_____

_____

_____

_____

_____

_____

PAPER 4 LISTENING COMPREHENSION about 30 minutes

FIRST PART

*For questions 1–6 put a tick in **one** of the boxes **A**, **B**, **C** or **D**.*

1   Edward Hall claims that nuclear power stations

   A have never caused fatalities.

   B provide almost three quarters of some countries' electricity.

   C are the safest way of generating even small amounts of energy.

   D produce completely harmless waste.

A	
B	
C	
D	

2   The caller is probably someone who

   A specialises in nuclear power.

   B is an expert in other kinds of energy production.

   C is a non-expert but is interested in the topic.

   D has never thought about the topic.

A	
B	
C	
D	

3   Hall says '. . . I'm afraid, Mr Stokes, . . .' to show that he

   A disagrees with him.

   B is frightened of him.

   C regrets what he has done.

   D is unsure of his facts.

A	
B	
C	
D	

4   When he says '. . . Well I'm sure your figures are right . . .', the speaker sounds

   A satisfied.

   B sarcastic.

   C doubtful.

   D indifferent.

A	
B	
C	
D	

5   The caller is in favour of

   A safer nuclear energy.

   B hydraulic energy.

   C coal produced energy.

   D none of these.

A	
B	
C	
D	

6   By the end of the conversation the caller feels

   A hopeful.

   B irritated.

   C bewildered.

   D intimidated.

A	
B	
C	
D	

SECOND PART

7   *Below are eight comments and five people. For each person there is **one** comment. Write the number of the comment in the box beside each person's name.*

1. NOBODY CARES ABOUT YOU HERE.

2. THEY LET ME DOWN.

3. THERE ISN'T ANY WORK AROUND HERE.

4. DO YOU WANT AN EVEN BETTER STORY?

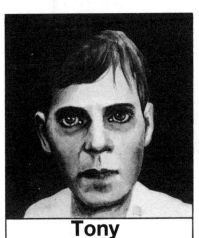

5. I WAS WASTING MY TIME AT HOME.

6. I WISH HE KNEW WHAT I LOOK LIKE NOW.

7. I GET SCARED IF I'M ON MY OWN.

8. THERE'S NOTHING I CAN DO ABOUT IT.

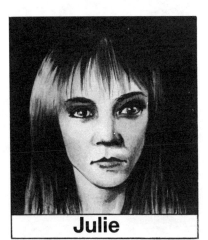

THIRD PART

*For questions **8–12** put a tick in **one** of the boxes **A**, **B**, **C** or **D**.*

8 The reviewer obviously dislikes the book. Which of these reasons does he **not** give?

    A Most of what it says is nothing new.

    B The information it contains is unreliable.

    C It could incite persecution.

    D It is part of an international conspiracy.

A	
B	
C	
D	

9 According to the reviewer, alien spacecraft

    A would be too heavy to leave their planet.

    B could only fly between planets, not stars.

    C could not reach the Earth.

    D would be too big to be kept secret.

A	
B	
C	
D	

10 The book claims that the aliens which have landed on Earth

    A have been seen by ordinary people.

    B are super-intelligent.

    C are better armed than Earth's governments.

    D might have been secretly murdered.

A	
B	
C	
D	

11 The reviewer says that stories of alien 'bases'

    A demonstrate the author's ignorance.

    B were widely believed 20 years ago.

    C have been disproved by American astronauts.

    D will not be believed by anyone.

A	
B	
C	
D	

12 The reviewer's attitude to the book is one of

    A sadness.

    B rage.

    C boredom.

    D contempt.

A	
B	
C	
D	

FOURTH PART

13 *For question **13** tick whether you think the statements are* **true** *or* **false**.

		True	False
a	The speaker wishes he could understand teenagers' TV.		
b	Children are speaking French to confuse their parents.		
c	The speaker thinks that G-language is difficult.		
d	G-language makes the communication of ideas quicker.		
e	Backslang has no connection with G-language.		
f	The speaker's name is Anthony.		
g	'Grommet' is a term of abuse.		
h	Some of the words should be comprehensible to adults.		

PAPER 5 INTERVIEW

The theme of this Test is **Reading**.

1   **a**   Look at *one* of the photographs and describe:
       □   the setting
       □   the people
       □   the books or newspapers

     b   Now discuss the relative merits of the following:
       □   hardback or paperback books?
       □   classics or modern literature?
       □   buying or borrowing books?

2 Study *one* of these passages. You may quote from it if you wish.

a Obviously I have a view of the world which is not theirs. I insist on my right to have that, and I insist on my right to express it as I see fit. It's very simple in this country. If you don't want to read a book, you don't have to read it.

b Publishers, especially male ones, are irritatingly complacent. It's a business that's very open to women, they'll say. True, but what happens to the women? While two-thirds of the profession is made up of women, only a fifth get directorships. Is that the new dawn of working womanhood? But with the coming sharp decline in school-leavers, publishing is going to have to nurture its staff, and especially its female employees. Demography may just achieve what the woman's lobby has tried so hard to do.

c The *New Musical Express*'s traditional irreverence will remain, but shorter features and plainer writing are anticipated, whilst its vigorously left-wing socio-political content will from now on be characterised by that most pregnant of euphemisms 'a more balanced approach'. After all, at the adult end of the rock demography, this is now the age of the rejuvenated Sixties dinosaur and its very own dream medium, the compact disc.

Where do you think the text is taken from?
Who do you think the speaker or writer might be?
What is the purpose of the text?
Discuss the content.

3 Do *one* of these tasks.

a Give your views on this statement:
'Technology will inevitably make books and other publications obsolete.'

b Which of these books would you like to read? Why?

Paperbacks

***Geniuses Together*, by Humphrey Carpenter (Unwin Hyman, £5.99).**
   Carpenter's enjoyable book chronicles the activities of the Montparnasse crowd – Joyce, Pound, Hemingway, Gertrude Stein and others – during the golden era of Modernism. A fascinating mix of literary references, anecdotes and evocative descriptions of the 'moveable feast' that was Paris in the 1920s.

***Women Novelists Today*, by Olga Kenyon (Harvester Press, £9.95).**
   Olga Kenyon's illuminating study of six contemporary women writers traces the dissemination of feminist ideals into mainstream fiction and considers the way in which individual writers have focused on – or chosen to ignore – questions of female autonomy in their work. Iris Murdoch, A. S. Byatt, Margaret Drabble and Fay Weldon are among the writers discussed.

***Myself With Others*, by Carlos Fuentes (Picador, £3.99).**
   Fuentes brings together autobiography – an account of the author's peripatetic childhood – and literary criticism. Essays on the formative influences on his own work (Cervantes, Borges) and on Latin American literature in general are interspersed with thoughts on the writer and totalitarianism.

TEST THREE

PAPER 1 READING COMPREHENSION 1 hour

SECTION A

In this section you must choose the word or phrase which best completes each sentence. **On your answer sheet***, indicate the letter* **A***,* **B***,* **C** *or* **D** *against the number of each item 1 to 25 for the word or phrase you choose.*

1 Until I hear a really convincing argument I'll _____ an open mind on the subject.

   A maintain   **B** have   **C** show   **D** keep

2 She knew that _____ that moment she was completely on her own.

   A in   **B** on   **C** by   **D** at

3 He's been arrested, but the police haven't _____ him yet.

   A processed   **B** charged   **C** convicted   **D** cross-examined

4 That's another job done; I'll cross it _____ the list.

   A from   **B** of   **C** off   **D** out

5 He may not be ideal, but when all's _____ and done there's no-one else.

   A said   **B** made   **C** thought   **D** finished

6 Take your driving licence with you _____ you get stopped by the police.

   A if   **B** in case   **C** provided that   **D** in that case

7 The court's decision is seen as a major _____ to their authority.

   A hit   **B** blow   **C** damage   **D** undermining

8 In the _____ of any clear leadership, the rebellion collapsed.

   A lack   **B** omission   **C** absence   **D** vacancy

9 I'm afraid we'll be away _____ when you come over.

   A for holiday   **B** for holidays   **C** on holiday   **D** on holidays

10 Now here's an _____ on the main news story we've been covering.

   A upshot   **B** update   **C** upgrade   **D** upturn

11 They struggled _____ the hurricane-force gusts that swept the pack ice.

   A for   **B** against   **C** with   **D** among

12 I'm a bit concerned _____ how the new law might affect our business.

   A in   **B** as   **C** for   **D** about

13 The planes were delayed and the hotel was awful, but _____ we still had a good time.

   A on the contrary   **B** by the same token   **C** on top of all that   **D** for all that

14 It was very _____ of you to send me such a lovely birthday present.

   A sympathetic   **B** mild   **C** obsequious   **D** kind

15 I'd just as _____ have a quiet meal at home as eat out.

    A soon   **B** rather   **C** well   **D** much

16 He has been in _____ ever since he was convicted of taking bribes.

    A shame   **B** disrepute   **C** reproach   **D** disgrace

17 What time's the _____ train to London?

    A latest   **B** last   **C** terminal   **D** final

18 They had a terrible row _____ who should do the housework.

    A on   **B** with   **C** over   **D** relating

19 Now _____ in the flour until the sauce thickens, and cover.

    A remove   **B** dump   **C** stir   **D** scramble

20 New peace proposals were _____ at the recent Middle East conference.

    A shown off   **B** spoken out   **C** put forward   **D** made up

21 The service is slow and the food's cold; it's the last time _____ here.

    A I have eaten   **B** I ate   **C** I'll eat   **D** I'll have eaten

22 We had no way of knowing what _____ ahead of us.

    A lay   **B** lied   **C** laid   **D** lain

23 The opposition parties have _____ for new measures to relieve poverty.

    A called   **B** demanded   **C** cried   **D** claimed

24 It was only a ten minute ferry crossing but the baby was _____ twice.

    A infirm   **B** sick   **C** poorly   **D** ill

25 It's still not _____ that the meeting will go ahead as planned.

    A sure   **B** definitive   **C** certain   **D** doubtless

SECTION B

In this section you will find after each of the passages a number of questions or unfinished statements about the passage, each with four suggested answers or ways of finishing. You must choose the one which you think fits best according to the passage. **On your answer sheet**, *indicate the letter* **A**, **B**, **C** *or* **D** *against the number of each item* **26** *to* **40** *for the answer you choose. Give* **one answer only** *to each question. Read each passage right through before choosing your answers.*

FIRST PASSAGE

Some years ago the Associated Press put out a glossary of the adjectives then fashionable for describing women in the American Press. 'Beautiful', as I recall, meant pretty. 'Pretty' meant attractive. 'Attractive' meant 'not positively repulsive' and 'voluptuous' (a great favourite at the time, along with 'svelte') meant overweight.

Now that the major cities are awash with glossy property magazines and free sheets supported almost entirely by the soaring prices of houses, a comparable conversion table is overdue. With inflated house prices comes inflated language. As an insatiable browser through the throwaways I know that the basic equations are commonsense. 'Garden flat' means a basement; 'patio flat' a basement with no garden, probably overlooking dustbins. A 'cottage-style' house is very small, and one on the 'Fulham-Chelsea border' is in Fulham.

But doing some legwork recently with an erstwhile first-time buyer, I learned the deeper nuances. 'Surprisingly quiet' means on a main road. 'Investment area' means a slum. So does 'near Tube', with the extra connotation of 'high crime area.' A 'penthouse' is the top flat in any building and usually has very small, high windows. A 'period feature' can be a bathtub with legs.

Most of these Yuppy-bait 'new conversions' have been fashioned out of old Victorian houses never intended to be carved up into flats. Hence 'extremely well modernised' means kitchen and bathroom crammed into two halves of a partitioned bedroom. And if the result is still so eccentric that no room has any logical function, then it is called 'extremely versatile accommodation'.

Poor Mr Walter Annenberg, when American ambassador in London, was mocked for referring to 'elements of refurbishment' at the embassy residence, but that was restraint indeed. Almost all of the property now coming on the market has been refurbished, usually in hideous ways that the new owner will find impossible to alter – but not to describe.

What cannot be altered must be endured and labelled 'potential'. 'Potential roof terrace' refers to any jutting ledge capable of supporting a tub of geraniums. A 'potential third bedroom' is a loft with no ladder. 'Incredible potential' means that even an estate agent's prose-artist cannot imagine how the place can be dragged into the 20th century.

26 The writer initially got her information for the property 'conversion table' from

   A her experience of seeing property.
   B advertising handed out in public places.
   C US newspapers.
   D expensively-produced specialist publications.

27 Which of these does the writer say she has actually seen?

   A A 'garden flat'
   B A 'patio flat'
   C A 'cottage-style' house
   D A 'penthouse'

28 Buildings described as 'new conversions'

   A are no longer in fashion.
   B are not used for their original purpose.
   C do not have separate rooms for cooking and sleeping.
   D waste a lot of space.

29 The expression 'elements of refurbishment' is

   A grammatically incorrect.
   B very informal language for a diplomat to use.
   C American English.
   D rather pretentious.

30 The writer suggests that owners will not find it difficult to describe refurbished property because

   A they will be familiar with words such as 'potential'.
   B they will probably not be foreigners.
   C it is so ugly that the words will come easily.
   D most of the property currently for sale is refurbished.

SECOND PASSAGE

War is hell but *War and Remembrance* (ITV) is worse. Even the baritone promos which have been filling commercial television for weeks give the project overtones of a natural disaster. 'In 1983,' the voice-over croaks, 'thirteen million people were swept away by *The Winds of War. . . .*'. If true, this would be a reversal of the usual process by which people sweep rubbish away. But despite having suffered this grim fate, the same 13,000,000 are expected to be swept back by this sequel, a further adaptation of the works of Herman Wouk. *War and Remembrance* is, the sound track growler promises, 'the greatest television event of all time.' This, you suspected, was probably a reference to the expense.

And so it proved, as the statistics began to spit: $100,000,000, John Gielgud, ten countries, Robert Morley, 32 hours of episodes, five years in the making. The last is the one which makes you gasp; the show took as long to make as the war did to fight. While you idly hope that the same team might now like to begin work on dramatising the 100 Years War with the same time ratio, it is with this fact that the nature of the project hits you. Usually, we look to war stories for a certain selection of key events, even reflection on their genesis and effects. *War and Remembrance*, however, has a different agenda. American television has simply restaged the Second World War, in its entirety. This is the action replay, 50 years on.

This sounds as if it ought to be symbolic and the making of *War and Remembrance* is indeed the perfect morality tale for peacetime media America. The fiction mirrored the fact to the extent that those who started the débâcle ended up saying never again. The 32 hours finished their run in the States short of audience and advertising.

Its bloated shape is not, though, the only problem with the piece. Sanitised family dialogue leads, for example, to a sailor saying 'the captain's scared out of his mind,' which was a disappointment after all you'd heard about salty naval talk. There is also Robert Mitchum. *War and Remembrance* is centred on a family called the Henrys. Those who were swept away in 1983 will remember that the head of the Henrys is Victor, known as Pug and played by Mitchum. In recent years, this actor's performances have increasingly had less to do with acting than with those nature documentaries in which a camera is pointed at a flower for a year in the hope of showing growth. Yet, even by those standards, his Pug is a miracle of impassivity. So little energy does Mitchum expend on characterisation that you keep thinking the camera has jammed. In the first 90 minute episode (only $30^{1}/_{2}$ hours to come), the Japanese, desperate to get a reaction out of Mitchum, hurled everything they had at the US fleet.

---

31 Which of these does the writer consider to be "rubbish"?

A Books by Herman Wouk.
B Advertisements for *War and Remembrance*.
C The programme *The Winds of War*.
D People who watched *The Winds of War*.

32 How long would the writer like the programme makers to spend on their next TV series?

A Five years.
B Twenty years.
C Fifty years.
D A hundred years.

33 According to the writer, *War and Remembrance*

A is not the kind of project the makers want to repeat.
B was highly successful in the USA.
C covers some of the incidents which took place during World War II.
D consists entirely of film shot in the 1940s.

34 The writer feels that, in the context, the phrase 'the captain's scared out of his mind,' is too

A mild.
B vulgar.
C informal.
D literary.

35 Which of these phrases expresses something the reviewer imagines?

A 'centred on a family called the Henrys'
B 'known as Pug and played by Mitchum'
C 'only $30^{1}/_{2}$ hours to come'
D 'desperate to get a reaction out of Mitchum.

THIRD PASSAGE

1 Alcohol has such wide and general effects on the body that the search for a complete remedy is probably doomed to failure. Remember that we are dealing here with the body's response to a chemical that is routinely used as a disinfectant, an industrial solvent and a pickling agent for biological specimens. You cannot expect to drink it with impunity. Prevention is better than cure and so the only real answer is to resist its charms. If it is already too late for homilies on abstinence and you cannot find a satisfactory placebo, then all you can do is learn to love your hangovers.

2 At last it looks as though the fashionable set are losing their bottle. First it was the no-alcohol lunch, as the fast-trackers discovered that business and booze don't mix. And now the trend is extending into evenings and weekends. The bright ones are cutting out alcohol completely, and teetotal is totally chic. For some, it's part of a rigid health regime. But for the majority it's an inevitable consequence of working hours that have spread over into leisure time, of business lunches that have become dinner discussions and drinks after work, and the need for young professionals to remain clear-headed and capable.

3 The time will come when you are stranded in some unspeakable hellhole on holiday, and all the bars are closed. Fellow travellers are emptying wallets and hocking watches for half bottles of the local rotgut. Meanwhile, up in your hotel room, out comes the duty-free bottle of your choice, and if the tap water looks rather too murky, neat liquor never really hurt anyone. An Australian colleague and I once nursed our airport Scotch through a dry election day in the outback of El Salvador. After a while, we agreed, you hardly noticed the bullets and bombs.

4 Empty champagne and wine bottles littered tables, normally reserved civic dignitaries turned into flirtatious lounge lizards and student guests became increasingly boisterous as they drank the free drink. It could have been any one of a thousand office parties, but for one extraordinary difference: there were no embarrassing faux pas, no breath test failures and no hangovers, because none of the drink that loosened tongues and swept away social barriers at the health authority function contained a trace of alcohol. When I told them all the champagne, wine and supposedly powerful punch they had drunk so copiously was non-alcoholic, the guests were stunned. Some of them became angry because they thought they had been cheated.

36 Which text contradicts text 1?

  A 2
  B 3
  C 4
  D None of them

37 How many of these texts refer to drinks which appear to be alcoholic but which in fact are not?

  A One
  B Two
  C Three
  D Four

38 Texts 2 and 4 agree that alcohol

  A is becoming less popular.
  B is incompatible with work.
  C makes human relations easier.
  D can affect one's judgment.

39 The purpose of text 4 is to show that

  A too much alcohol can make even responsible people behave badly.
  B enjoyment of alcohol is psychological, not physiological.
  C office staff have a tendency to drink too much.
  D it is very easy to become addicted to alcohol.

40 Which text replies to a reader's letter asking for advice?

  A 1
  B 2
  C 3
  D 4

PAPER 2 COMPOSITION 2 hours

*Write **two only** of the following composition exercises. Your answers must follow exactly the instructions given. Write in pen, not pencil. You are allowed to make alterations, but make sure your work is clear and easy to read.*

1 Describe the personal possession you would most like to have. (About 350 words)

2 'The Cold War ended with the opening of the Berlin Wall.' Discuss.
(About 350 words)

3 Write a story which ends as follows: 'It was awful, but it was no less than he deserved'.
(About 350 words)

4 You are investigating a case of alleged discrimination by employers.

The applicant for the job claims that s/he was rejected in spite of having both better qualifications and greater experience than the other candidate, and believes the personnel manager was prejudiced against him/her.

The personnel manager claims that the application was given scrupulously fair consideration, but that the other candidate gave a better interview.

The advertisement was headed as follows:

> ## **EQUAL OPPORTUNITY EMPLOYER**
>
> Applicants are considered on the basis of their suitability for the post, with equal opportunities for women, black/ethnic minorities, and people with disabilities, regardless of marital status, age, creed/religion and unrelated criminal conviction. All posts are open for job-sharing.

Write **two** contrasting reports for the Equal Opportunities Commission based on the evidence given by

a the rejected applicant,

b the personnel manager.
(About 150 words each)

5 Set books

PAPER 3   USE OF ENGLISH   2 hours

SECTION A

1   *Fill each of the numbered blanks in the passage with **one** suitable word.*

Crime isn't rising because the laws are not strict enough, or because the sentences are not tough

enough, or _____(1) because there aren't enough policemen _____(2) the beat. It is

rising because the agencies and individuals who can _____(3) a preventative effect on crime

are not pulling together or in the same _____(4). The police are _____(5) of those

agencies, of course. But crime prevention is also a matter for governments who are content to

_____(6) mass unemployment turn _____(7) a way of _____(8), for councils

who _____(9) to shout yah-boo at the police instead of getting _____(10) with

making life safer for local people, for architects who _____(11) exposed and indefensible

buildings, for parents who don't take enough interest _____(12) what their teenage children

are _____(13) up to and for householders who sit inside and moan _____(14) than

do anything _____(15) the state of the neighbourhood or the street. _____(16)

prevention had been neglected for too _____(17) by too _____(18). Over the last ten

years it has been wilfully neglected _____(19) defiance of mounting evidence that it is the

central hope of effective action _____(20) crime.

2   *Finish each of the following sentences in such a way that it is as similar as possible in meaning to the sentence printed before it.*

Example: It wasn't easy to find the house.
Answer: We had *difficulty finding the house.*

a   Since he couldn't move it himself, he asked for help.

   Not _____

b   I would really hate to have to work night shifts.

   Working _____

c   Somebody was observing every move he made.

   His _____

d   We spent more time talking about it than actually doing it.

   Talking _____

e   There is no risk of contamination at any stage of the process.

   At no _____

f None of the sacked workers have been reinstated.

The management _____

g If you do not pay you will be prosecuted.

Failure _____

h The most amazing aspect of the crime was its sheer audacity.

What _____

3 *Fill each of the blanks with a suitable word or phrase.*

Example: As usual, there are two sides ___*to the*___ story.

a In no way _____ blame for what happened.

b She _____ back yet or she'd have phoned by now.

c Had his brakes been working properly _____ crashed.

d The dining room looks so much better since you _____ up.

e They don't stand _____ beating us in the final.

f At his age he _____ better than to behave like that.

4 *For each of the sentences below, write a new sentence as similar as possible in meaning to the original sentence, but using the word given. This word **must not be altered** in any way.*

Example: He had no idea what to say.
        loss
Answer: *He was at a loss for words.*

a What a surprise it was to see her there!
fancy

_____

b Why do you get so angry about such trivial incidents?
fuss

_____

c They can't afford the deposit, not to mention the instalments.
let

_____

d He looks exactly like that man on television.
spitting

_____

e Do write me a short letter when you get there.
line

_____

f Her reaction was not really surprising.
came

---

g Only a relatively small area was affected by the outbreak.
confined

---

h Please reply to this letter immediately.
return

SECTION B

5 *Read the following passage, then answer the questions which follow it.*

For 25 years now, Jane Goodall has been studying chimpanzees in the wild, at Gombe in Tanzania. After ten years she wrote her best-selling book, *In The Shadow Of Man*, chronicling her research until then. But if she had stopped there she would have left the world with a misleadingly benign view of chimpanzees.

For it was always thought that one of the most important divisions between the human species 5
and all others was our viciousness, our unique and universal habit of making war upon one another, a savagery unknown in the animal kingdom. The only species with a moral sense was also the only species that deliberately destroyed others of its own kind.

But starting in the early seventies, Jane Goodall and her researchers were horrified to observe a prolonged, deliberate and planned warfare by one group of chimpanzees upon another group which 10
had broken away some years previously. It fundamentally altered her perception of chimp society as ordered and peaceable. It also brought them, in her eyes, yet closer to homo sapiens.

Her most startling discovery in her early years was that chimps use tools. Until then, palaentologists made sharp distinctions between tool users and non-tool users to differentiate between men and monkey. She documented and photographed chimps taking long sticks, poking 15
them into termite holes, and extracting the termites on the sticks in order to eat them.

At the same time she and other researchers discovered that chimps are the only animals, apart from humans, to be self-aware. At its most primitive level this can be demonstrated by sticking something on a chimp's forehead and showing him a mirror. The chimp will immediately recognise himself and pull the object off his forehead. Other animals will paw at the mirror and fail to 20
recognise themselves, let alone rearrange themselves according to the image in the mirror. They also have a structured language with abstract concepts.

But her clinical and dispassionate description of the war that obliterated a whole chimp community may change our perceptions again of the closeness of the relationship between them and us. 25

There was, it appeared, no particularly pressing reason for the larger northern group to set about annihilating the southern group. They turned against the other group because in the years since the two groups parted, they had become aliens, and, like humans, chimpanzee groups are hostile to those outside the immediate group. She observed too that many of them, especially the younger males, took deliberate pleasure in seeking out danger, by ranging close to the territory occupied by 30
other groups. One or two especially aggressive animals were first to head in the direction of alien chimp calls, and last to linger near a potential fight. Despite the scientific language, the characters of some of these aimlessly belligerent young males stand out like street-fighting gangleaders.

a   Give another expression for 'in the wild' (line 1).

_____

_____

b   How long ago did Goodall write her book?

_____

c   Explain in your own words why it is fortunate she carried on with her research.

_____

_____

d   What is meant by 'viciousness' (line 6)?

_____

_____

e   How did the 'warfare' (line 10) change Goodall's opinion of chimpanzees?

_____

_____

f   What is the purpose of the reference to 'long sticks' (line 15)?

_____

_____

g   What differentiates chimps from other animals?

_____

_____

h   Explain the experiment designed to demonstrate this.

_____

_____

i   In what way is our view of chimps likely to be altered as a result of Goodall's research?

_____

_____

j   Explain the expression 'set about annihilating' (lines 26–27).

_____

_____

k   Why did the groups fight?

_____

_____

l   What did some chimps enjoy doing?

_____

_____

m   Explain what the 'especially aggressive animals' (line 31) did.

_____

_____

n   What is meant by 'aimlessly belligerent' (line 33) and why does the author refer to 'street-fighting gangleaders'?

_____

_____

o   In a paragraph of 60–80 words, summarise the similarities between chimp and human behaviour.

_____

_____

_____

_____

_____

_____

_____

_____

_____

_____

_____

_____

_____

PAPER 4 LISTENING COMPREHENSION (about 30 minutes)

FIRST PART

For questions 1–9 fill in the missing information on the map and in the boxes below. For questions 3, 7 and 8 on the map use the key to help you.

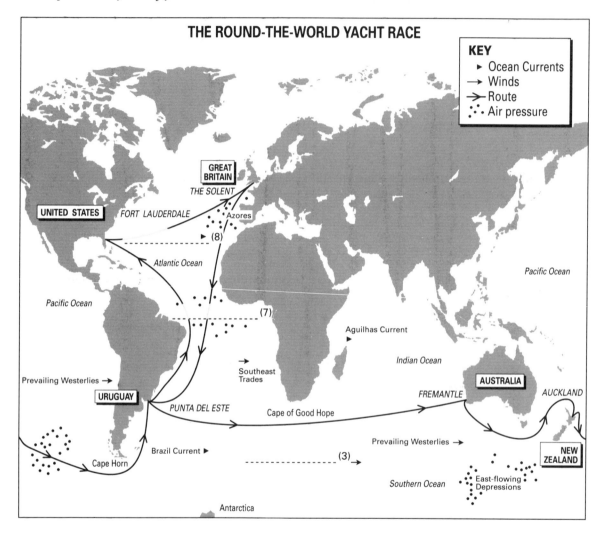

THE ROUND-THE-WORLD YACHT RACE

KEY
- ▶ Ocean Currents
- → Winds
- ⇉ Route
- ∴ Air pressure

GREAT BRITAIN
THE SOLENT
UNITED STATES
FORT LAUDERDALE
Azores
(8)
Atlantic Ocean
Pacific Ocean
(7)
Aguilhas Current
Indian Ocean
Pacific Ocean
Southeast Trades
Prevailing Westerlies →
URUGUAY
PUNTA DEL ESTE
Cape of Good Hope
FREMANTLE
AUSTRALIA
AUCKLAND
Brazil Current ▶
Prevailing Westerlies →
(3) →
NEW ZEALAND
Cape Horn
East-flowing Depressions
Southern Ocean
Antarctica

Dates	
------------------ (1)	Depart from The Solent
9th – 18th Oct:	Arrive in Punta del Este
28th Oct:	Depart from Punta del Este
------------------ (4)	Arrive in Fremantle
23rd Dec:	Depart from Fremantle
12th – 16th Jan:	Arrive in Auckland
------------------ (5)	Depart from Auckland
28th Feb. – 8th Mar:	Arrive in Punta del Este
17th Mar:	Depart from Punta del Este
18th – 21st Mar:	Arrive in Fort Lauderdale
5th May:	Depart from Fort Lauderdale
------------------ (9)	Arrive in The Solent

Distances

1st leg
The Solent – Punta del Este _____ miles (2)

2nd leg
Punta del Este – Fremantle   7325 miles

3rd leg
Fremantle – Auckland   3430 miles

4th leg
Auckland – Punta del Este _____ miles (6)

5th leg
Punta del Este – Fort Lauderdale   4161 miles

6th leg
Fort Lauderdale – Solent   3837 miles

SECOND PART

*For questions **10–14** tick **one** of the boxes **A**, **B**, **C** or **D**.*

10 The earliest valuable records mentioned are from the

    A 1950s

    B 1960s

    C 1970s

    D 1980s

A	
B	
C	
D	

11 A non-stereo copy of *Please Please Me* might now be worth

    A £150

    B £200

    C £400

    D £2000

A	
B	
C	
D	

12 The target for *Spiral Scratch* is to sell

    A more copies than *Record Collector* did three years ago.

    B more copies than *Record Collector* does now.

    C the same number of copies as *Record Collector* did three years ago.

    D the same number of copies as *Record Collector* does now.

A	
B	
C	
D	

13 The increasing demand for collectable records means that

    A the shop price of new singles is going up.

    B fairly quick profits can sometimes be made.

    C covers are becoming more expensively-produced.

    D old singles are being released again.

A	
B	
C	
D	

14 Which of these is the most valuable?

    A *Express Yourself*

    B *Laughing Gnome*

    C *The Third Degree*

    D *God Save the Queen*

A	
B	
C	
D	

THIRD PART

*For questions 15–17 tick **one** of the boxes **A**, **B**, **C** or **D**.*

15 The colour of the sky as seen from very high up is caused by

    A lots of very small particles in the air.

    B high-altitude clouds.

    C the very clean air.

    D the light being scattered.

A	
B	
C	
D	

16 The air pressure inside a plane flying at 38,000 feet is

    A similar to that at the top of the Himalayas.

    B the same as the external pressure at 10,000 feet.

    C equal to that at the Earth's surface.

    D higher than that at the Earth's surface.

A	
B	
C	
D	

17 Which of these is given as a possible reason for the unusual cloud formations seen by passengers?

    A other aircraft

    B features on the Earth's surface

    C following winds

    D the direction in which they are flying

A	
B	
C	
D	

FOURTH PART

18 *For question 18 tick which of the following advertising slogans will be allowed.*

    a   THE GOVERNMENT COULDN'T CARE LESS   ☐

    b   YOU DON'T NEED THE DETAILS TO KNOW IT'S HELL   ☐

    c   WILL YOUR CONSCIENCE ALLOW YOU *NOT* TO GIVE?   ☐

    d   VERY MUCH A PERSON – VERY LITTLE LUCK   ☐

    e   ALL WE ASK IS A FEW COINS FROM YOUR POCKET MONEY   ☐

    f   CHARITY BEGINS AT HOME – NOT IN ANOTHER CONTINENT   ☐

    g   500 LANDLORDS REFUSED HER A HOME   ☐

    h   TRUST US TO SPEND YOUR CONTRIBUTION WISELY   ☐

PAPER 5 INTERVIEW

The theme of this Test is **Relationships**.

1 **a** Look at *one* of the photographs and describe:
  ☐ the setting
  ☐ the people – particularly their expressions and body language
  ☐ their likely feelings towards each other

  If you are doing the interview in a group, contrast the impression given by the people in your picture with those in the others'.

  b Now discuss:
  ☐ the reasons why people are attracted to one another
  ☐ how they show it
  ☐ the factors which make a successful relationship

2   Study *one* of these passages. You may quote from it if you wish.

a   Many young people of sort of around nineteen think that the 1960s were really wild days – but when you actually explain to them that in fact their relationships and practices are probably much more outrageous than than um they were in the sixties I think they're actually quite they're actually quite surprised. I mean they actually live much more according to what really were the sixties' values than I think we did in the 1960s.

b   Tell her – and you'll probably lose a friend. There's always the chance, you see, that she *knows* what's going on and is turning a blind eye to it. Relationships are pretty complicated and if they're broken up/made up several times there must be something there to hold them together. It's her relationship. Even though you feel things aren't right, you can't interfere. Just let her know you're around – and be there with the box of Kleenex when she needs it.

c   The close relationship between health and happiness is a long established theory. I would take it a step further in saying it's an indisputable fact. And yet how often does your doctor enquire into the state of your personal relationships? Keep your eyes open. Don't shun the attentions of other men if you're ensnared in an unfulfilling relationship. Your health and happiness are too important!

Where do you think the text is taken from?
Who do you think the speaker or writer might be?
What is the purpose of the text?
Discuss the content.

3   Do *one* of these tasks.

a   Choose role A, B or C and discuss the problem with the examiner or other candidates.

Role A
You are worried that your partner is not taking your relationship seriously enough – you've been told that he/she's been seen out with other people.

Role B
You are very fond of your partner but think he/she's rather possessive – you want to get to know other people and feel you're too young to settle down with anyone yet.

Role C
You are a good friend of both partners and think they are very well suited in most respects – but unless they can understand each other better you feel the relationship might break up.

b   Discuss these advertisements. Which person sounds the most interesting?

VERY ATTRACTIVE FEMALE (22) graduate but non-careerist, tired of independence and living alone, seeks sincere, affectionate, educated man to share life with. Photo please. Box No 10569.

LOVELY BLONDE LADY EXEC. (25) – cultured, educated, good sense of humour – currently disillusioned with the male species – perhaps you can persuade her otherwise? Box No. 8369.

MALE, MID TWENTIES, seeks slim, fairly attractive female, 20–25, 5′3″ to 5′9″ for galleries, concerts, films, walks, chat and who knows ... Box No. 10769.

IF YOU'RE BORED WITH LIFE then answering my ad. will change things, I promise. Handsome, charming man, 22, seeks lively, attractive woman for good times. Photo, phone no. please. Box No. 6769.

TEST FOUR

PAPER 1   READING COMPREHENSION   1 hour

SECTION A

In this section you must choose the word or phrase which best completes each sentence. **On your answer sheet**, *indicate the letter* **A**, **B**, **C** *or* **D** *against the number of each item 1 to 25 for the word or phrase you choose.*

1 I don't know whether you'll succeed, but at least _____ a go at it.

   A have   **B** try   **C** make   **D** do

2 It's freezing outside; you'd better _____ black ice when you drive home.

   A look down on   **B** check up on   **C** watch out for   **D** keep out of

3 That looks more like _____ of the pen than a gap in her knowledge.

   A a slip   **B** an error   **C** a fault   **D** a mistake

4 No-one's even studied the problem, _____ tried to do anything about it.

   A not to say   **B** far more   **C** in no way   **D** much less

5 Recent events have _____ doubt on the minister's judgement.

   A thrown   **B** cast   **C** meant   **D** raised

6 Steps are to be taken to _____ overspending in the public sector.

   A quell   **B** curb   **C** crush   **D** quit

7 The new model is quite an improvement _____ its '80s predecessor.

   A to   **B** in   **C** for   **D** on

8 Parents are demanding an immediate _____ on drug pushing near the school.

   A crackup   **B** breakdown   **C** crackdown   **D** breakup

9 Cosmetics are by far the most _____ side of our business; $12 million this year.

   A beneficial   **B** profitable   **C** monetarist   **D** interesting

10 He was sitting on his own in the pub, feeling very sorry _____ himself.

   A about   **B** for   **C** to   **D** with

11 One of the survivors tells how she was _____ by falling masonry.

   A beaten   **B** knocked   **C** clubbed   **D** struck

12 As soon as she finished her _____, she began to look for her first job.

   A career   **B** degree   **C** study   **D** master

13 If you interrupt the witness again, you will be held to be in _____ of court.

   A scorn   **B** disdain   **C** derision   **D** contempt

14 The suspected terrorist was _____ to the police at the border crossing.

   A handed over   **B** handed in   **C** handed out   **D** handed on

15 The government now expects a $10 billion _____ in revenue, so taxes will have to go up.

    A fallout   **B** shortfall   **C** shortcoming   **D** outcome

16 The pilot managed to land the plane _____ following the mid-air explosion.

    A securely   **B** surely   **C** safely   **D** certainly

17 The _____ leader of the deposed junta is to face trial for corruption.

    A former   **B** prior   **C** foregoing   **D** late

18 There seems to be little hope _____ rescuing the company from collapse.

    A for   **B** in   **C** about   **D** of

19 The nursing staff are exhausted; they've been _____ all weekend.

    A on call   **B** on guard   **C** on line   **D** on patrol

20 We watched helplessly as the same thing happened all _____ again.

    A fully   **B** over   **C** completely   **D** through

21 At the third attempt, he finally succeeded _____ the world championship.

    A to win   **B** in winning   **C** winning   **D** to winning

22 If we go ahead with this scheme, the _____ line is that we'll have to find $1 million from somewhere.

    A first   **B** top   **C** bottom   **D** last

23 We are extremely strict _____ food hygiene in our kitchens.

    A with   **B** around   **C** about   **D** throughout

24 When he finally decides to do something, he usually makes a good _____ of it.

    A attempt   **B** effort   **C** work   **D** job

25 Rumours of further military unrest were _____ following the abortive coup attempt.

    A rife   **B** extended   **C** plentiful   **D** global

SECTION B

In this section you will find after each of the passages a number of questions or unfinished statements about the passage, each with four suggested answers or ways of finishing. You must choose the one which you think fits best according to the passage. **On your answer sheet**, *indicate the letter* **A**, **B**, **C** *or* **D** *against the number of each item* **26** *to* **40** *for the answer you choose. Give* **one answer only** *to each question. Read each passage right through before choosing your answers.*

FIRST PASSAGE

Back in October 1884 a conference was held to draw up the world's time zones. But it also agreed on the near-universal adoption of a device that then seemed of manifest good sense, and which came to be called The International Date Line.

This Line, which was drawn to rid calendars of an annoying duality whereby those journeying long distances from East to West found they had lost a day of their lives, and those going in the opposite direction discovered they had an extra one, was initially set down almost arbitrarily in the middle of the Pacific Ocean.

It could have been established just about anywhere. I believe there is a case to be made, now that the Pacific has become unquestionably the most important ocean in the world, that the Date Line should be moved.

It should be erased from its present, uncomfortable-looking position and re-sited in an almost arrow-straight line, with most of its length coinciding with the 30th meridian west of Greenwich. And that is slap bang in the middle, not of the Pacific, but of the Atlantic Ocean.

Such a shift would cause problems, true. Those who shuttle between London and New York would find their lives strangely disrupted. But I venture that those doing business between the Thames and the Hudson are a steadily dwindling band, fast being replaced by a richer and more energetic crew who are dealing between the Far Occident and the Far Orient. Since these latter hold the key to the world in their hands, their convenience should be of more consideration than that of their passed-over colleagues on the old Atlantic. The easing of business across the Pacific would be of inestimable value to the world as a whole, and would far outweigh the trifling inconvenience of having Monday become Sunday on a jet flight over what the blasé like to call 'the Pond'.

Just imagine. At present, when it is noon on Monday in Hong Kong it is, we are presently taught to think, sixteen hours behind in Los Angeles. It is, in other words, 8pm on Sunday. But if the Date Line were not there at all those of us in the East could more reasonably think of Los Angeles as being eight hours ahead of us – it would still be 8pm, but on Monday, the same day as ourselves. And in such a situation it would not be at all unreasonable to suppose that the international bankers working over in California would be in their offices, and keen to do business with the East. Everyone would be sharing the same day. No problem.

26 The aim of the 1884 conference was to

- **A** show where Western time ended and Eastern time began.
- **B** ensure the date remained the same for West to East travellers.
- **C** decide what time it would be in different parts of the world.
- **D** ensure the date remained the same for East to West travellers.

27 The position of the Date Line in the middle of the Pacific

- **A** was a very sensible decision.
- **B** was immediately accepted everywhere.
- **C** caused confusion for Trans-Atlantic travellers.
- **D** was a choice made without good reasons.

28 The author proposes moving the Date Line to a position

- **A** East to West, straight across the Atlantic.
- **B** East to West, virtually straight across the Atlantic.
- **C** North to South, straight down the Atlantic.
- **D** North to South, virtually straight down the Atlantic.

29 Why does the author propose the change?

- **A** Trading between Europe and East Asia would become easier.
- **B** The financial centres around the Pacific are increasingly important.
- **C** It would be afternoon both in the Western Pacific and on the US West coast.
- **D** Transatlantic travellers are mostly ageing show business stars.

30 The author is at present in

- **A** Hong Kong.
- **B** Los Angeles.
- **C** New York.
- **D** London.

SECOND PASSAGE

What would it mean if we actually did discover the ultimate theory of the universe? As was explained in Chapter 1, we could never be quite sure that we had indeed found the correct theory, since theories can't be proved. But if the theory was mathematically consistent and always gave predictions that agreed with observations, we could be reasonably confident that it was the right one. It would bring to an end a long and glorious chapter in the history of humanity's intellectual struggle to understand the universe. But it would also revolutionize the ordinary person's understanding of the laws that govern the universe. In Newton's time it was possible for an educated person to have a grasp of the whole of human knowledge, at least in outline. But since then, the pace of the development of science has made this impossible. Because theories are always being changed to account for new observations, they are never properly digested or simplified so that ordinary people can understand them. You have to be a specialist, and even then, you can only hope to have a proper grasp of a small proportion of the scientific theories. Further, the rate of progress is so rapid that what one learns at school or university is always a bit out of date. Only a few people can keep up with the rapidly advancing frontier of knowledge, and they have to devote their whole time to it and specialize in a small area. The rest of the population has little idea of the advances that are being made or the excitement they are generating. Seventy years ago, if Eddington is to be believed, only two people understood the general theory of relativity. Nowadays tens of thousands of university graduates do, and many millions of people are at least familiar with the idea. If a complete unified theory was discovered, it would only be a matter of time before it was digested and simplified in the same way and taught in schools, at least in outline. We would then all be able to have some understanding of the laws that govern the universe and are responsible for our existence.

31 The ultimate theory of the universe

   A could be accepted if based on objective, tested criteria.
   B might have been discovered a long time ago.
   C was discovered a long time ago but has yet to be tested.
   D would need conclusive proof to be accepted.

32 Discovery of the right theory could mean

   A people would lose interest in the nature of the universe.
   B having to establish new laws to explain the universe.
   C reversing a trend which began after the time of Newton.
   D ordinary people understanding subsequent modifications to it.

33 Nowadays, who has a basic understanding of all human knowledge?

   A Science students at university and scientists.
   B Scientists.
   C Scientists working only in particular areas.
   D Nobody.

34 A complete unified theory would

   A enable everyone to understand the general theory of relativity.
   B only require a degree in science to understand.
   C be understood to some extent by many ordinary people.
   D make humans act more responsibly.

THIRD PASSAGE

Four extracts about being small:

1 Mighty Mouse

If you thought this first section was going to be a regurgitation of that old chestnut about mice terrifying elephants, you can relax. As it happens, elephants do tend to be afraid that rodents might run up their trunks – but it is highly likely that the humble mouse once played a far more significant role in the history of the world.

Various theories have been put forward to explain why the dinosaurs died out 65 million years ago, such as: raids by hunters in flying saucers; a lack of room in Noah's Ark; a lemming-like mass suicide by all species everywhere at the same time; and even 'Paleoweltschmerz' (i.e. the dinosaurs became so disillusioned with their world that they died of sheer boredom).

However, a somewhat more plausible reason for their extinction is that small shrew-like mammals ate their eggs.

2 The lowest of the low

The person who has come the closest to being a twelve-inch ruler is Attila the Hun. He is thought to have been a dwarf. For a time he ruled jointly with his elder brother Bleda (who was actually quite a big Bleda by comparison), but he found this rather inconvenient and he murdered him in 445.

His hordes then massacred, looted and burned their way across eastern Europe and finally assailed the Roman Empire. He was defeated once – in Gaul in 451 – but he promptly invaded northern Italy and occupied the imperial palace in Milan, where he had all the paintings altered to show the Roman emperor kneeling at his feet instead of vice versa.

3 Le petit caporal

No one had as great an effect on Europe again until Napoleon Bonaparte came to prominence at the end of the eighteenth century.

In 1795, at the age of 25, he was in charge of the French army of the interior. He then led the French forces in Italy to brilliant victories over the Austrians and had himself crowned Emperor in 1804.

In defeating the Austrians, incidentally, he also defeated the hero of our first section. The Austrian generals became so desperate that they inked a mouse's feet and placed it on a map to see if it would trace out a path to victory. It didn't.

Yet without his wellingtons on, Napoleon was only five feet six inches tall himself. It is true that he looks impressive in that most famous of paintings, which shows him crossing the Alps in 1800 on a white charger, but this is a highly idealized portrait. (For one thing, he actually crossed on a mule.)

4 The pocket battleship of the desert

T.E. Lawrence or 'Lawrence of Arabia' actually measured less than five feet six inches, but this tends to be obscured by the fact that the tall Peter O'Toole played him in the David Lean film.

After joining the Arab army in 1916, the archaeology scholar soon became its chief organising and motivating force. He ran a guerrilla operation against the Turks, blowing up numerous bridges and trains, and in 1917 he captured Aqaba after a 600-mile march.

Further successful actions followed, and when Lawrence returned to Britain as a colonel in 1918, he was awarded the DSO and the Order of the Bath – though he declined both honours as a protest against the breaking of promises made to the Arabs.

35 Who was the shortest?

    A Attilla
    B Bleda
    C Napoleon
    D Lawrence

36 Stories about mice frightening elephants are

    A false.
    B nauseating.
    C exciting.
    D clichéd.

37 Which is entirely serious in tone?

    A Section 1
    B Section 2
    C Section 3
    D Section 4

38 Which refers to a character in another section?

    A Section 1
    B Section 2
    C Section 3
    D Section 4

39 Which refers to a deliberate act of falsification by order of the subject?

    A Section 1
    B Section 2
    C Section 3
    D Section 4

40 The aim of the advertisement is to show that

    A determination brings success
    B competition is a natural instinct.
    C lack of size is not a drawback.
    D biggest means worst.

PAPER 2 COMPOSITION 2 hours

*Write **two only** of the following composition exercises. Your answers must follow exactly the instructions given. Write in pen, not pencil. You are allowed to make alterations, but make sure your work is clear and easy to read.*

1   Describe the rudest person you have ever met. (About 350 words)

2   Why does rock music play such a large part in many young people's lives? (About 350 words)

3   Write a story which begins as follows: 'I knew that if they didn't see me, I had a good chance of escaping' (About 350 words)

4   Write the texts for **two** of the recorded messages referred to in the following advertisement: (About 150 words each)

DEAL WITH YOUR PROBLEMS BY RINGING A FRIEND

Just call 346 9573 followed by the number you want and listen to Lifeline's advice. All messages are recorded by warm and caring people who are speaking from experience.

Calls charged at 25p per min. cheap rate, 38p per min. at all other times.

Emotional Problems

101   Giving up smoking

103   Coping with exams

107   Overcoming shyness

111   Drug dependence

114   I don't like my appearance

116   Drinking too much

120   Beating insomnia

123   He's left me for someone else

124   She's left me for someone else

LIFELINE

PAPER 3   USE OF ENGLISH   2 hours

SECTION A

1   *Fill each of the numbered blanks in the passage with **one** suitable word.*

The food industry has promised to deliver the weight-watcher's fantasy – a fat-free fat to

_____(1) butter and margarine. The no-calorie spread, which could also be _____(2)

in cakes and biscuits, is being developed by Proctor and Gamble. Early tests _____(3)

overweight Americans have produced phenomenal results. Volunteers who turned _____

(4) for trials at the University of Cincinnati lost _____(5) average of 8lb in 20 days after

swallowing 2oz of the fat substitute daily, _____(6) to a report in the Journal of the

American Medical Association.

   What _____(7) the no-calorie spread even more remarkable is that it is made from a

combination of nature's _____(8) waistline-busters – sugar and fat. By a trick of chemistry,

up _____(9) eight fatty acids molecules are attached to a sucrose (sugar) molecule in the

middle. _____(10) reasons not fully understood, this manmade confection, _____

(11) as 'sucrose polyester', is completely indigestible and, so, calorie _____(12). Some

studies even suggest that it also works _____(13) a sponge, soaking _____(14)

cholesterol eaten in other fatty foods.

   The idea of enjoying gluttony _____(15) guilt of girth does not please _____(16).

Mr Michael Jackson, who runs the Center for Science in the Public Interest, a Washington-based

consumer _____(17), said: '_____(18) all the money the food industry would make

if we all _____(19) buying twice as many cookies and cakes without putting _____

(20) weight.'

2   *Finish each of the following sentences in such a way that it is as similar as possible in meaning to the sentence printed before it.*

Example: It's about to become the top-selling model.
Answer: It's on *the point of becoming the top-selling model.*

a   The water was too deep for him.

   He was out _____

b   She was quite exhausted by the demanding timetable.

   She found _____

c   Only Alain Prost has won more Formula One races.

With the _____

d   They have little in common but still get on very well together.

Despite _____

e   The company lost a substantial amount last year.

The company made _____

f   An early announcement is doubtful.

It is _____

g   'We are spending more on education than ever before', he claimed.

He claimed that more _____

h   The roses were the only plants to survive the frost.

Apart _____

3 *Fill each of the blanks with a suitable word or phrase*

Example: You won't find that book anywhere. It's ___*out of*___ print.

a   She was just standing there. It was _____ seen a ghost.

b   By the end of the race, he _____ runners behind.

c   The rain forests are vanishing. If we do nothing, by the year 2000 many species

_____ out.

d   I was really hungry and the delicious smell _____ mouth water.

e   Would you be so good _____ a lift to the station?

f   She is really looking _____ taken out to dinner.

4 *For each of the sentences below, write a new sentence as similar as possible in meaning to the original sentence, but using the word given. This word **must not be altered** in any way.*

Example: Please write on alternate lines.
        other
Answer: *Please write on every other line.*

a   He shouted as loudly as he could, but nobody heard him.
top

_____

b   They asked the boss to increase their salaries.
rise

_____

c It's about time we began.
made

_____

d The roof needs mending, not to mention the walls and woodwork.
nothing

_____

e The police car crashed while chasing a stolen vehicle.
pursuit

_____

f I find it hard not to spend more than I earn.
ends

_____

g He was highly offended by the story that appeared in the press.
exception

_____

h Which settlers arrived first?
arrive

_____

SECTION B

5 *Read the following passage, then answer the questions which follow it*

Raymond Dank is crouching in the kitchen of his dark, malodorous pothole described by estate
agents as a basement flat. A fog of cigarette smoke hangs in the air. In front of him on the formica-
topped table is an ashtray overflowing with stubbed-out Marlboros and a smeared half-empty
whisky glass. Around him are piles of yellowing newspapers that were once an acre of Norwegian
forest. Dank looks at his watch. He is late for a dinner party at Clive and Cynthia Vertue's docklands 5
duplex. Hastily he inspects his burgeoning wine rack and seizes a choice bottle of powerful Barolo,
stuffed full of tannin and artificial colouring. Leaving the flat, he grabs his potent aerosol 'air
sanitiser' and jets an ozone-hostile blast behind him to annihilate all known odours and airborne
bacteria while he is out. For good measure, he ambushes his cat and showers it with a good blast of
highly toxic flea spray (also deadly to the ozone layer). Outside, his ageing Renault Five is dripping 10
oil onto the street. He leaps in, pulls out the choke and emits a stifling cloud of lead-abundant
exhaust gas as he roars off in search of adventure, pausing only to empty his choked ashtray on to
the pavement behind him.

Raymond Dank is not the sort of guest you and I welcome these days. He is walking death to the
planet, a one-man band of toxic effluent, and – worst of all – he has no compunction about the 15
damage he's doing to other people's environment. The only good thing about him is that we can all
feel superior to him, because we've all given up the things he still does every day.

Clive and Cynthia Vertue certainly feel superior to him. They are already apologising for him to
their other, more caring guests.

Arriving with his bottle of additive-friendly red, Dank immediately pulls out his pack of Marlboro, 20
cheerfully observing that no one will mind if he smokes. There is a shocked silence. Everyone else
has, naturally, given up. 'I'm sorry, Raymond,' says Clive softly. 'But we do rather mind, actually.
There is a significant risk of getting lung cancer from passive smoking, you know.'

They sit down to dinner. Dank's bottle is uncorked and passed round the table. One by one, the
right hand of each guest flies up over the glass. 'I've given up red, actually'; 'I don't drink any more 25

on weekdays'. Piggish and obscene, Dank slugs down his brimming red in solitary, brutish indulgence.

Renouncing the world used to be popular with those about to enter fulltime religious instruction. But its appeal has spread lately. Everyone is busy giving up activities which, until now, were a normal part of human behaviour. It is not enough simply to stop using, say, drink or cigarettes or biological washing powder. 'Giving up' has taken on the fervour of religious conversion. Those newly converted to the refusal of tap water or artificial preservatives find it necessary to broadcast their self-denial at every opportunity. Even worse, they excoriate those who are still drinking themselves to death or polluting the environment. The mere act of 'giving up' confers the illusion of moral virtue. If you've given something up, you can't help feeling you are a better person than poor old Raymond Dank, still yielding to his baser, animal appetites.

a What is meant by 'overflowing with stubbed-out Marlboros' (line 3)?

b What does the writer mean when she says that the newspapers 'were once an acre of Norwegian forest' (lines 4–5)?

c Who or what is 'stuffed full of tannin' (line 7)?

d Explain the phrase 'jets an ozone-hostile blast' (line 8).

e Give another expression for 'For good measure' (line 9).

f What does 'roars off' (line 12) mean and why is it appropriate here?

g What is meant by 'walking death to the planet' (lines 14–15)?

h What are 'more caring guests' (line 19)?

i Why is there 'a shocked silence' (line 21)?

j Explain the meaning of the phrase 'passive smoking' (line 23)

k What happens when they sit down to dinner? What excuses do they make?

l   Explain the phrase 'slugs down his brimming red' (line 26)

_____

m   What does 'its' refer to on line 29?

_____

n   What similarities are there, according to the text, between 'giving up' and 'religious conversion'?

_____

_____

o   In a paragraph of 70–90 words, summarise the criticisms of Raymond Dank.

_____

_____

_____

_____

_____

_____

_____

_____

_____

_____

_____

_____

_____

_____

_____

_____

_____

PAPER 4 LISTENING COMPREHENSION (about 30 minutes)

FIRST PART

1 *Tick whether you think the following statements are **true** or **false**.*

	True	False
a Professor Larson loses his temper when he has to queue.		
b The first research on queueing was done by Larson.		
c The longer the delay, the angrier people inevitably get.		
d Delays are particularly annoying for people who need not wait for luggage.		
e At Houston airport, luggage now reaches the reclaim faster.		
f People most resent what they see as unfairness.		
g If passengers are told the truth, they get even more enraged.		
h The computerised bank was forced to work more efficiently.		

SECOND PART

*For question **2** you must complete the missing information in boxes **1–6** beside the map. Some of it has been filled in for you.*

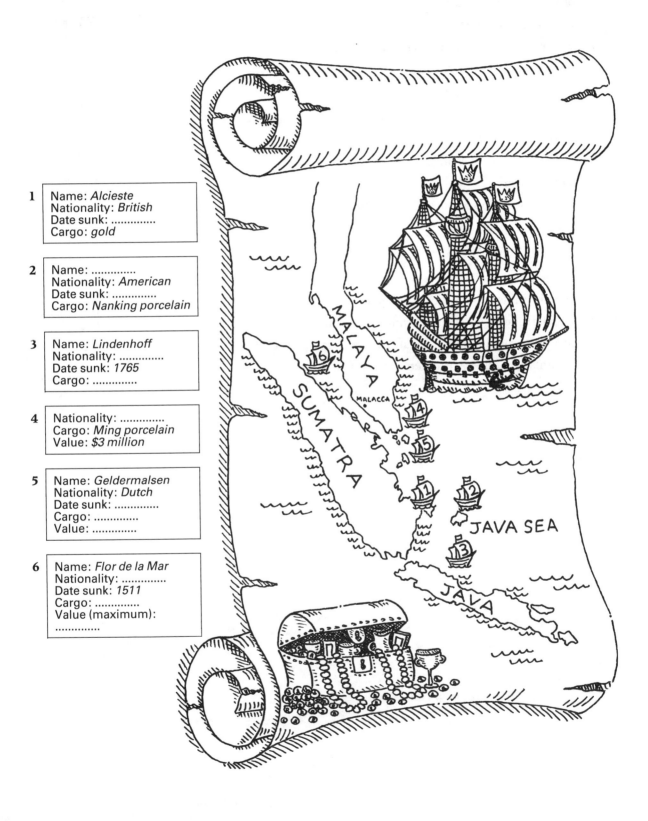

1
| Name: *Alcieste* |
| Nationality: *British* |
| Date sunk: .... |
| Cargo: *gold* |

2
| Name: .... |
| Nationality: *American* |
| Date sunk: .... |
| Cargo: *Nanking porcelain* |

3
| Name: *Lindenhoff* |
| Nationality: .... |
| Date sunk: *1765* |
| Cargo: .... |

4
| Nationality: .... |
| Cargo: *Ming porcelain* |
| Value: *$3 million* |

5
| Name: *Geldermalsen* |
| Nationality: *Dutch* |
| Date sunk: .... |
| Cargo: .... |
| Value: .... |

6
| Name: *Flor de la Mar* |
| Nationality: .... |
| Date sunk: *1511* |
| Cargo: .... |
| Value (maximum): |
| .... |

THIRD PART

*For questions 3 and 5 tick **one** of the boxes A, B, C or D. For question 4 tick the appropriate boxes a–f*

3 According to the presenter, mobile phones
   A are the status symbol of the future.
   B will bring about a revolution in telecommunications.
   C have increased the number of traffic jams.
   D are becoming less popular.

A	
B	
C	
D	

4 Which of the following things do mobile phone users complain about?
   a non-essential calls
   b the impossibility of changing their phone number
   c physical pain
   d the fear of missing commercial opportunities
   e interrupted meals
   f the high cost of making calls

5 The major phone dealers say that
   A nobody wants to be without their phone.
   B 'cellular fatigue' is a relatively minor problem.
   C customers could transfer unwanted calls to someone else.
   D it is unfair that their customers are sent to jail.

A	
B	
C	
D	

FOURTH PART

*For questions **6–8** tick **one** of the boxes **A**, **B**, **C** or **D**.*

6   Kevin's tone of voice at the beginning of the interview suggests he is

   A   worried.

   B   confident.

   C   sad.

   D   confused.

A	
B	
C	
D	

7   Kevin asks 'Do you have to. . .' because he

   A   wonders whether Marian has been told to mention the topic.

   B   doesn't know what she is going to say.

   C   is embarrassed by what she is going to say.

   D   thinks the interviewer will not be interested.

A	
B	
C	
D	

8   Throughout the interview, Marian's tone is

   A   hurt.

   B   sceptical.

   C   complaining.

   D   aggressive.

A	
B	
C	
D	

PAPER 5 INTERVIEW

The theme of this Test is **Animals**.

1   **a** Look at *one* of the photographs and describe:
    - ☐ the setting
    - ☐ the dog
    - ☐ the person

   b Now discuss
    - ☐ the reasons why people have dogs
    - ☐ the drawbacks of having one
    - ☐ legal controls on dogs and their owners

2   Study *one* of these passages. You may quote from it if you wish.

a   I was sickened by a recent article on the killing of rats in the Sudan. These intelligent, sociable animals are our fellow mammals. Like us, they sometimes breed too plentifully for their own good and compete with us for scarce food supplies. This can be tragic for both species, but ultimately rats are far less destructive of this planet than we are.

b   I might make a film about a walk through the jungle – a film lasting, say, half an hour: and in that film there will be 10, 20, 30 different species of animals that will miraculously appear from around me. But if you go to a jungle, you might walk for days without seeing a single bird or monkey. Then you will realise to what extent natural history film-makers such as me have distorted reality. But a 30-minute film about a jungle where nothing happens is not really what you turned the television set on to see.

c   He was eight feet long. At the centre of his back he was two feet in circumference. Slipping sinuously along the bottom of the sea at a gigantic pace, his black, mysterious body glistened and twirled like a wisp in a foaming cataract. His little eyes, stationed wide apart in his flat-boned, broad skull, searched the ocean for food. He coursed ravenously for miles along the base of the range of cliffs. He searched fruitlessly, except for three baby pollocks which he swallowed in one mouthful without arresting his progress. He was very hungry. (Liam O'Flaherty *The Conger Eel*)

Where do you think the text is taken from?
Who do you think the speaker or writer might be?
What is the purpose of the text?
Discuss the content.

3   Do *one* of these tasks.

a   Prepare a talk on one of these topics:
  ☐ The usefulness of animals to human beings.
  ☐ Animal rights.
  ☐ A famous animal in history.
  ☐ Hunting or fishing.

b   Look at the advertisement below. Try to persuade the examiner or other candidates to go.

Could this be your ancestor?

Have you wondered about one of your relatives? Have <u>they</u> ever wondered about <u>you</u>? Are we descended from these great beasts who once roamed our earth? Come and find out:

Museum of Archaelogy and Natural Science, Great London Road, SW4

SAMPLE COMPOSITIONS

The titles of the sample compositions are taken from the tests in this book. The compositions were written by CPE candidates and marked by experienced Paper 2 examiners. Each composition was marked by all the examiners and the marks and comments which follow represent a consensus of their assessments.

Because the examination is a test of language ability as a whole, the candidate does not pass or fail each paper individually; if he/she is weak in one paper of the exam, the Examinations Syndicate considers that he/she will be similarly weak in other papers as well. So it should be noted that, although a mark of 8 or more out of 20 for an essay indicates a pass, the candidate's performance in Paper 2 is compared with his or her performance in the other papers. If these marks are not all more or less the same, then the candidate's performance will be looked at more closely to make sure than no examiner has made a mistake and marked too high or too low. The examiner's performance is also compared with all the other examiners', so that this subjective part of the examination is as fair as possible.

You may like to look at these compositions with the marking scales in order to appreciate the level required by the examination.

MARKS AND COMMENTS ON THE SAMPLE COMPOSITIONS

Test 2   page 38   *Christina*
Describe the laziest person you know

I guess the laziest person I know must be my best friend Kan back home. We met each other at school and we have known each other for many years though it was not till we started college that we became best friends. We are very different from each other Kan and I, sometimes I really wonder how we can stay as close as we do.

She prefers to stay at home, do as little as possible while I always like to be up and around, do everything that comes into my mind Though we do have very little in common we always have and always will be the best of friends, the reason is simply because she is herself.

Though Kan is a very lazy person she is ever such a lovely girl and she has very much to give a friend. She is a person to whom you can always talk to whatever the subject is, and you know, she knows, but no one else. You can always trust her, she will always bee there when you need someone, provided you get in the car and make the visit. After living in England for a year, she has not paid a visit, no phone call only a couple of post cards and letters. dissappointing many would say. Well, at first I thought so too till we met again and I saw nothing had changed, it was just as if I had never left at all. When things are like that I do not mind having a lazy friend like her, a friend whom you have to drag out of the house to the disco, pub cinema or where ever you want to go.

When you look at Kan you see a lovely natural girl, there is never any fuss with her. Yes, she is a bit over weight becaue she is to lazy to be bothered with exercise, but in many ways it fits her, it is part of her personality. Her flat looks more like a wearhouse, tidy up is something she does once a month she just can not make the effort to any more than that. Do not ever give her flowers, she will not water them and they will die within a couple of weeks. This is just her, she is as lazy as you can imagine and I think it is hard to find someone like her

Examiners' comments

This composition is very clearly planned and well-written. It is substantial, natural-sounding and interesting. The few errors are minor, being mostly concerned with spelling and punctuation. However, it was felt that the candidate was not as ambitious as might be expected at this level.

Mark 16

Though we are so very different Kan and I, she will always be my best friend. And it is not only really difficult to have a relationship like that, the only thing is you have to learn to respect the other person for what she/her are. Sometimes you have to struggle to get them out of the door, but you also have to give way and respect their decision to stay at home. Kan is very lazy, the laziest person I know, but the is clean, friendly and honest and thats what counts!

Test 3 page 56 *Susanne*
Write a story which ends: 'It was awful, but it was no less than he deserved.'

He looked around carefully. It was dark and no one could be seen. He went on opening the door with a crowbar and with a certain noise it opened. As soon as he stepped into the hall the alarm went off, But it was no problem, for he knew where the machine was and tapped in the code number.
She was all alone in the house and awoke by the sound of the alarm.

'Oh no' she thought,
'not another false alarm!'

She went downstairs to the machine and all of a sudden, in the same moment as the alarm stopped, she saw him.

'Now what are you doing here? I told you that I didn't ever . . .' she stopped, seing the gun in his hand. She was just about to say something, when he fired.

'I'm sure you'll never see me again!' he went upstairs and took the jewels out of her jewellery case.

'That's worth 5.000 bucks at least!'
He laughed.

In the middle of his laughter he heard a police car approaching. He got nervous and left the house in a hurry.

He was just coming out when the police car stopped in front of the house. He ran away.

'Stop! Police!' said one of the officers, while the other went inside the house. When the policeman had discovered her, he phoned for an ambulance and then the two policemen followed him.

He had been ahead enough to hide in the nearby circus where a performance was taking place.

The first person he saw happened to be the lion trainer. He hit him on the head and stole his costume. But it was high time the performance of the wild lions started. So what other choice did he have than to behave as if he was the trainer and just do it.

'The lions are probably very nice' he thought.

But the lions noticed at once that something was wrong and that is was not the man they were used to. So, in order to protect their terretory they attacked and killed him.

Two days later she was well enough to have an interview with the two police officers. She had been wounded seriously but not fatally.

When hearing the news about her ex-lover all she could say was 'It is awful, but it's no less than he deserved'.

Examiners' comments

This composition flows well and is highly entertaining. It is accurate and shows a consistent use of tenses. However, the style is rather simple, and not quite polished enough to justify a higher mark.

Mark 15

Test 3 page 56 *Luigia*
Describe the personal possession you would most like to have.

There is nothing on the earth I crave for more than having my blue Siemese cat back! I had one of those two years ago and it died. As it was a lady, and I loved it so much, I will address to it with she, reptectfully.

Who dares to claim that cats love their houses rather than their families? I have never known a more loyal friend in my whole life than that prettiest, loveliest cat. When everybody let me down, she was there to cheer me up with her kisses and purrings. She sympathetically stared at me with her huge blue eyes, glimmering in her small little face. She looked at me as if she wanted to utter human words of comfort and, in the effort, she sweetly mieawed.

She had a minute body, very agile though, and she could make incredible jumps. Not only did she reach the highest tops of the furniture, but she could walk along the edges with amazingly steadiness as well. She used to follow me, step by step, whereevere I went, jumping around me joyfully. When she fell pregnant and gave birth to eight sweetest kittens, she still never interrupted to follow me. It was a hard work to carry eight kittens, whenever I moved to a different room, but she bravely managed it.

She was a responsible mother as much as a best friend, and she attended her duties fulfillingly.

She was four years old when she caught a bad illness, which consumed her slowly and painfully. She couldn't eat any more, and, whenever she managed to swallow some food, she rejected it at once.

She died, and I am still suffering when I remember her, as she appears vividly in my mind.

I feel guilty, because I was too careless with her. I wish I had her back beyond any rational thought, beyond the thought that she cannot live again.

This composition is both an entertaining and effective realisation of the task. It is well-planned and there is a clear progression of thought. However, there are a few basic problems with articles and adverbs, superlatives and prepositions.

Mark 13

Test 1 page 18 *Danuya*
'Religious intolerance is on the increase.' Discuss.

Who has ever said that one religion is better than the other? If it is so, how is it measured, weighed or estimated? It seems that the idea as such is a pure nonsense. In the same way that the world is divided into people of different colours of skin, different nationalities or different classes, we are also divided into different religious groups. We inherit certain beliefs in almost the same way we inherit money or property and what we do with them depends entirely on ourselves. Therefore, there are people who, at some point in their lives, stop practising any sort of religious rituals but still claim to be believers; then, there are those who drop out of their spiritual groups completely having come to the conclusion that they do not need such unearthly practices. Finally, there are sound believers who keep up with what they preach and are quite happy about it. Yet, among all of them there are also those who are more than ordinary believers – they are religious fanatics.

Fanaticism, in its multitude of forms, has accompanied man throughout the ages. The stay-at-home orators – be it royals, clergymen or politicians – always found fools to be ready to go (if necessary) and fight and die for the cause. 'Down with popery', 'Fight the heathens' – in the past as well as in the present, seem not only to remain popular but even gain in status. For a fanatic, whoever is of an opinion other than himself, as far as the Godly realm is concerned, is a potential enemy. It is all the more threatening nowadays than it

The candidate has written a fluent and well-thought out composition. The argument and the examples are clearly thought out. However, the task is not entirely achieved, and a whole section is irrelevant. There are some problems with articles and vocabulary. The use of paragraphing is not always adequate.

Mark 13

was in the past as contemporary societies claim to have reached a higher stage in their developement. In what sense, one may ask, and the question will be justified. Oral abuse, stone throwing, devastating properties of religious opponents certainly do not speak in favour of such a state of affairs. It is true we are ready to enter the 21st century: we have conquered space, we have reached much of what had once ben considered unattainable, but, yet, we have not been able to come to terms with our religious opponents. The moon, then, is, by all means, ours, but in our hearts we have not made a single step forward. We are still ready to kill in the name of God.

The communist intolerance of religious beliefs is supported by the 'might is right' approach and therefore churches are being closed, public worshipping abolished, legal actions undertaken against those who disobey. Irish Catholics and Protestants resort to street killings and bombing, shooting around with complete disregard for the age of their victims. One religious group have passed a death sentence on a man who dared to express or interpret his view on the teachings of a holy book. They all maintain they only are right and if people happen to die in the process it only serves them right (the opponents, of course).

One often wonders if it is not true that thirst for bloodshed is humans' second nature. There seem to be a thousand and one excuses to kill another man. This is, perhaps, why wars are a never-ending business. But, for God's sake, let's not allow emotions to overcome common sense. To err is human but let's make an end to it at last.

Test 2   page 38   *Felix*
Write the story of an event which changed the course of your country's recent history.

1990: the eighties are over now; is there a better moment to look, in retrospect, at the most relevant events of the decade . . . even though we focused on Spain's recent history, there would be too many to be written down on a 350 words composition. Then, If I had to choose one event which had changed the course of Spain's recent history, I would choose the entry into the EEC (now the EC!); as an event, it is difficult to describe, for it was (at least at the beginning) a mere adhesion treaty: it is the consequences of this treaty that will really matter.

On January the first 1986, there was, in the streets, this typical mediterranean atomosphere of joy and merriment mingled with the smell of commemorative 'povios', the never ending toasts (some ending in noisy carousals), and flags, thousands of flags.

At this time, I was in London, and as I watched the events on the 'nine o'clock news', I couldn't realise how much would change in the Iberian Peninsula . . .

Since that day, Europe didn't end at the Pyrenees anymore, Spain is no longer different and 38 million people feel, at last, they are European again. A politician would have said that, with this meeting with its natural European dimension, Spain closed a long chapter of its history in which the introversion of its problems made it loose the pulse of history; the truth is that after a long period of isolation, we were 'back at home'. Should we remember that, some centuries ago, we didn't need to fight to belong to Europe, for Europe belonged to Spain . . . !

Four years later, I can see things are beginning to change, slowly though: still, Spanish are noisy, dirty and irrespectful towards nature; the number of newspapers is on the increase, not the number of readers not the quality of infor-

Examiners' comments

This is a well-planned composition and the ideas are clearly expressed. There are however a few basic errors, and the style is not very natural. There are some problems with register and the candidate occasionally gets lost through being too adventurous.

Mark 9

mation; new highways are being built, but there are more accidents; Spain has more international reputation, but many americans still think we are somewhere at the other side of Rio Grande . . . Anyway, I'm hopeful about the future, and I'm concerned that this event will be remembered for being the first step of Spains modernisation

Test 3   page 56   *Denise*
Describe the personal possession you would most like to have.

There exist many things I would like to have, such as a house to live in, a good car, nice and fashionable clothes and expensive and exclusive jewellery. It is difficult to decide between all these things and some of them might be only a dream for my whole life. However, what is the point in having personal possessions? Do they make us happier? Some people want to gain things all the time. Moreover they are unhappy when they haven't got what they want and nor are they when they got it. This is very sad and I think our very high social standard is for a great deal to blame on it. People should learn to appreciate what they have got, instead of looking for and worrying about what they don't have.

It is quite common that people think personal possessions are essential and the only key to a happier life. Buying goods gives a satisfaction, but how long? How quickly are we worn off with a new item and watch out for something beter or else? Isn't it easy to envy someone, because he seems to have something what we still don't have. It is a pity how poor most of the minds are in our world.

What about good health, friendlyness, happyness and living in abundance? Many of us take all that for granted and they are astonished as well as baffled when they realise that they can't buy a feeling. Some of them try hard, but they will never mangage to be happy. I don't say that I am not like that, but I am aware of it and I try to see things in another way. That is why I chose happyness as the personal possession I would most like to have. I have already been successful and developed that I can posess the whole world through happyness. Not only is it something that noone can take away from me, but also the greatest ability of mankind. If only it would be with me all day for the rest of my life!

Examiners' comments

This composition is not a clear realisation of the task because it spent too long discussing the merits of possessions and did not directly answer the question until the last paragraph. There are spelling mistakes and problems with word order. With its numerous direct questions, it is rather elementary in style. However, it is just good enough to merit a minimal pass.

Mark 8

Test 2   page 38   *Manos*
Write the story of an event which changed the course of your country's recent history.

Such an event is the coming to power of the Socialist party after the elections of 1988. It is obvious that at that time things in this country went caring or seemed to, judging by the high percentage of votes this party won in these elections, over 48%.

To the success of this party contributed also the fact that it was a recently founded party with new for the most part, leaders. which were quite unknown to the general public. This made it possible to make themselves believed about the importand changes and improvements they were going to bring in all the sectors of public life throughout the country. Besides people tend to trust always somebody who gives them a hope and promises for better days particularly if her is a good demagog.

Unfortunately a few years later things didn't turn out right. There was a change indeed but to the worst, at least for the great majority fo the pop-

Examiners' comments

The content of this composition is good and it answers the question. But there are a lot of errors and word order problems, and the use of prepositions is sometimes shaky. The candidate fails in attempts to use complex sentence patterns and his control of tenses is not sure.

Mark 7

ulation. Promices were far from coming true. Very far from meeting people's expectations who felt a deep deception. But what is worst is the fact that the new government and the leaders of the party in power, proved to case exclusively about their continuity to power and regardless of the rising of prices of goods and the frauds they were involved in, they showed that they would go to any lengths to manage to be reelected and stay in power (encouraging them to harmful to society attitude like not paying taxes etc) to please them and win their votes.

What I dislike more in this party is the inconsistency its leader has shown in many occasions which make him a very unreliable person. I understand that this happens in politics but I think he is overdoing it.

I have no hesitation in affirming that the change in the course of my country's recent history was to the worse as definitely can see of any improvement brought about in the last ten years. On the contrary I see a general deterioration of the quality of our lifes and of our standard of living. What is more I see also a degradation of our general ethics and sense of values.

Test 2   page 38 *Maria*
Describe the aspects of society which you feel have got better or worse since you were a child.

Society hasn't changed very much since I was a child because I am only seventeen years old and, in my opinion, these aren't enough years to produce great changes.

However when I was younger, I can still remember, people weren't so materialist, I mean, nowadays people are very worried to have many things and lots of money. This is the reason which makes us selfish: we forget there are some people who can't have any house, car, food . . . The difference between social statements is becoming bigger: rich people is richer each day while poor people is poorer. I think a few years ago people were more worried about general notions like justice, freedom, democracy . . . Nevertheless as we have them now, we don't appreciate what we have; we think all these things have always been there and we don't realise all the efforts some people had to do to get them.

But not all the changes have been bad. Nowadays Spanish society has total freedom. After Franco's dictatorship, democracy has brought many changes. Repression finished while freedom took its place. People lost their fears and dared to express their ideas. In my opinion this is one of the most changes of our story.

Finally I'd like to remark one change which has been the most recent one. It is the situation of Spain in the world. Spain is included in many international organizations which means that we have a better economical and social level than a few years ago. Our society can enjoy more things: multinational companies, lots of new products . . . Distance between countries is becoming smaller: West world and east one have just formed an only one. Nevertheless, there are still great differences between third world and the industrial one. It will take a long time to finish with them.

To sum up, the biggest changes of our society (specially the Spanish one) have been: the increasing of materialism, the end of dictatorship and the beginning of democracy and, finally, the important situation of Spain in the world. I'm sure society will continue changing in next years; and I hope this change will be for good.

Examiners' comments

There are some good ideas in this composition. It answers the question in a reasonably natural way. However, there are some basic mistakes: a less than adequate knowledge of tenses, and difficulty in the formation of plurals. The candidate also has some problems with prepositions and articles. It needs to be more formal and less like spoken English.

Mark 6

Test 4   page 77   *Mary*

Write a story which begins 'I knew that if they didn't see me, I had a good chance of escaping.'

— 'I knew that if they did not see me I had a good chance of escaping' said the criminal that the police caught, with some help, few days ago.

— I suppose you were carelless replied the other criminal, who was in the same jail.

— But what went wrong in your plan?

— Well it is a long story.

— Do not worry, we have plenty of time!!!

— Everything started about a month ago. I was charged and convicted for kidnapping. The sentence they gave me was 15 years. But I was not so stupid to sit for 15 years in jail. So the day after they put me in jail, I start thinking an escaping plan. You see the whole idea was to manage to pass the rocks that surounded the prison without been seeing.

— Yes, but how would you manage to get to the nearest island?

— I was a very good swimmer and in jail, luckily, I did not lost my strength. In a few days I manage to carry to my joul a hammer and a long piece of metal which was like a screw-driver but fater and hardener and which I made especially for this purpose.

—But where.

— I know, you want to ask me where did I get all these? I used to work as a blacksmith in the jail. So it was very easy for me. And then I start work. I was trying to break the briks and the stones that were used to built the prison, by using the hammer and the piece of metal. I, tried not to make noise by putting at the top of that piece, my shirt. It was very difficult because I had to watch out the guards. After a week or so I managed to finish.

— How did you cover the hole you made?

— Oh, that was very easy. I just changed the position of my stuff, in a way that they could cover the hole

— And then?

— Then I arranged the day, or the night I guess to escape I waited until 11 and then I took my stuff away from the whole I was not afraid of the guards, because they had just passed and I had half an hour to leave the jail. As soon as I left, I start going down. When I finally dive into the sea they had already find out that I had escaped and they were looking for me, with torches. But I did not notice a boat with two fishermen which was behind me, in a not far distance. When they heart all that noice they understood what had happened and they start coming towards me. I start swimming but it was helpless. They caught me with a net, after all they were two, as if I were a fish. So they gave me back to the police. And here I am again. But they did not see me, I had a good chance of escaping.

Examiners' comments

This composition does not achieve the task set. It is a dialogue and not a story. The candidate demonstrates a very poor knowledge of the various tenses, punctuation and comparatives. The style is extremely elementary.

Mark 4

SAMPLE INTERVIEWS

The sample interviews can be heard on the cassettes accompanying *THE COMPLETE PROFICIENCY PRACTICE TESTS*. The material used in the sample interviews is taken from the four practice tests. The interviews took place in exam conditions and were conducted by experienced Paper 5 examiners. Like the sample compositions, they are designed to give both students and teachers an idea of the level required for success in this paper. They should **not** be seen as model interviews, either on the part of the candidate or on that of the examiners.

Since the examination is a test of language ability as a whole, candidates do not pass or fail each paper individually. The candidate's performance in this paper is compared with his/her performance in the other four papers, and if necessary, the final grade is adjusted accordingly. However, a mark of three or more in each of the six scales (see pages 9–10) would suggest that the candidate is of a suitable level to be successful in the exam. As with Paper 2, the examiner's own performance is under scrutiny. If the grades given to the batch of candidates interviewed by a particular examiner are consistently higher or lower than the candidates' performance elsewhere in the examination would suggest, then the grades may be adjusted.

You may want to listen to the sample interviews, while looking at the material used, and then mark the candidates using the scales. There are two people present during the interviews: the interviewer, who leads the discussion, and the assessor, who marks the candidates. In the examination itself it may not always be possible to have two examiners present. **Please note that because the recordings were made in authentic conditions, the quality of the sound may vary.**

First interview: Antonella and Akiko
Test 1   pages 24–25   Traffic

	Akiko	Antonella
Fluency	3	3
Grammatical accuracy	2	2
Pronunciation: sentences	3	3
Pronunciation: sounds	3	3
Interactive communication	3	3
Vocabulary resource	3	3

Second interview: Jacqueline
Test 2   pages 44–45   Reading

Fluency	4
Grammatical accuracy	3
Pronunciation: sentences	4
Pronunciation: sounds	3
Interactive communication	4
Vocabulary resource	4

Third interview: Huang Me and Barbara
Test 3   pages 62–63   Relationships

	Huang Me	Barbara
Fluency	2	3
Grammatical accuracy	2	2
Pronunciation: sentences	2	2
Pronunciation: sounds	2	1
Interactive communication	2	3
Vocabulary resource	2	2

Fourth interview: Sebastian
Test 4   pages 82–83   Animals

Fluency	2
Grammatical accuracy	2
Pronunciation: sentences	3
Pronunciation: sounds	2
Interactive communication	3
Vocabulary resources	2

The marks in the fourth interview are those given by the interviewer rather than those given by the assessor. In the event of any disagreement in the examination itself, the assessor is allowed to overrule the interviewer.

LISTENING SCRIPTS

TEST ONE: First part

You will hear a radio programme about minimalist music and art. Look at questions 1–6. For each question tick one of the boxes A, B, C or D. You will hear the piece twice.

Presenter: These bizarre musical innovations didn't come from nowhere. Nicholas Kenyon traces them back to the work of the American composer John Cage:

Kenyon: In 1952, Cage produced his highly controversial piece *4 minutes 33 seconds*, in which nothing happened except a pianist coming onto the stage, sitting at a piano for four minutes thirty-three seconds and then leaving the stage; and Cage was making the point there that the content of this piece, such as it was, was created by the audience, by extraneous sounds, by any hums, ha's, coughs, splutters, murmurs of protest and so forth, and I think that in . . . in absolutely stripping everything that we regard as musical away from music, made a very important point which the New York performance artists of the sixties took up with a vengeance. There was a whole group of them dedicated to what we would regard as . . . as nonsense events: pieces which had the text 'draw a straight line and follow it' or pieces which had as an instruction to a string quartet to come on and shake hands, and that was the piece.

Presenter: In the artistic ferment of 1960s New York, Cage was also an inspiration for sculptors and painters. Minimalist works of art are usually sculptures made of simple units, often in some industrial materials; the most famous is *Equivalent Eight*, by Carl André, which involves 120 house bricks arranged in a set order on the gallery floor. Richard Francis, of Liverpool's Tate Gallery, explains that minimal art, like minimal music, was meant as a challenge to the establishment.

Francis: It had a certain political bias at the time; because the artists were also looking for ways of making democratic art – I mean the high point of minimal art I suppose is 1968, or thereabouts; they were looking for an art that . . . that would be . . . um incapable of being sold in the galleries that . . . that the dealers would not be able to make a lot of money out of their art: they tried it first with conceptual art where things were written on pieces of paper, and then they moved into objects – and of course the dealers, as always, managed to subvert the process and minimal art is now extremely expensive, and . . .

Presenter: How much is, say Carl Andre's pile of bricks, one of his piles of bricks, how much is that now worth?

Francis: I think the last quoted price in the newspaper the other day was something like $80,000.

Presenter: Over the past 20 years, minimal music too seems to have been embraced by the establishment. Concerts of music by Steve Reich and Philip Glass attract large audiences. Reich's latest pieces are ambitious orchestral works, and Glass has taken to writing opera. David Bedford:

Bedford: The processes which they've set up . . . they're now regarding those as accompaniments, and putting melodies on top; so that Philip Glass, obviously using the human voice has got to write melodies for the human voice to sing: and often a sort of weakness is exposed in that they are not very brilliant melodists, because they're on this . . . this rhythmic impulse and hallucinary thing that goes on for ages and ages and ages, changing very slowly: to put a melody on top of that, you're setting yourself up for comparison with the great melodists of the past: Mozart, Wagner, Brahms and so on. So there's a slight problem at the moment for minimal composers – how to progress from now on.

Presenter: So if the experimental, pioneering phase of minimalist composition is past, isn't minimalism effectively over as a creative force? Nicholas Kenyon of *The Observer* believes not:

Kenyon: No, I don't think it's over. What is happening is that minimal music, if you like, is now aiming at maximal audiences; it's become a very popular art form, and in the process, you could argue that it has been modified to such an extent that it's lost a lot of its initial purity and clarity, but I think anybody can still tell the difference between an opera by Philip Glass, or, to take the most recent and . . . er highly successful example John Adams's opera *Nixon in China* – you can easily tell the difference between that and Puccini, so to that extent minimalism still has an identity and I think will go on having one for the foreseeable future; it represents a particular strand in the music of our time.

Now listen to the piece again.

TEST ONE: Second part

You will hear an extract from a radio programme called **New Ideas**. *Look at questions* **7–10**. *For each question tick one of the boxes* **A**, **B**, **C** *or* **D**. *You will hear the piece twice.*

Presenter: . . . and we've been looking out especially for things that make it easier to do various jobs. To start off then, David Hayes, let me try out something that grips onto the edge of your paint can to help you hold it for long periods.

Hayes: This product is actually basically a can-grip, so it's a convenient way of actually holding the can for you. So you've got a nice pistol handle here, to make a nice comfortable container and you basically get a number of rings that come with that, so it can hold a one-litre, a three-quarter or a half-litre can.

Presenter: Right, it's got a ring that grips the can . . . er it's in this black and yellow colour, and then a pistol grip for your hand and on top you've got this bit of plastic here the shape of a . . . a 'V' like a kind of clip – that's where the brush goes is it?

Hayes: That's right, I mean normally when you . . . the phone rings, you put the brush on the top of the can and . . . er you pick it up and you get covered in . . . in the paint, so this clips on the top so the drips actually fall into the middle of the can, and you keep the handle clean. So your hands are totally clean all the time.

Presenter: How much does it cost?

Hayes: You're talking about under £4.

Now listen to the piece again.

TEST ONE: Third part

You will hear three interpreters talking about their work. Look at questions **11–16**. *For each question tick one of the boxes* **A**, **B**, **C** *or* **D**. *You will hear the piece twice.*

Woman 1: It's been said that you can't translate culture so it's impossible to do so with language. It may be a valid point. But at the very least you've got to know the cultural background of the languages you're working into and out of: for English this means the British Isles, the States, Canada, Australia and so on, and for Spanish – even when you're working in Europe – you've got to understand the cultural references to Latin America, and so on.

Man: Yes, yes it's no good trying to interpret word-for-word, particularly sayings, and proverbs and the like, which are used a lot more in some languages than in others. For instance, in Greek it's 'to take the snake out of the hole', in German 'to get the cow off the ice' and although the idea of overcoming difficulties in the French 'to pull the chestnuts out of the fire' is close to the English sense, we tend to refer to someone else's chestnuts.

Woman 2: Yeah the point is that you can always get the idea across even if it means using a stock phrase to cover the huge range of adages that express one notion: something like . . . um 'a wise man does not play leapfrog with a unicorn'

Woman 1: But jokes can be a nightmare can't they, I mean there's a gap that seems like ages between the laughter from the people who understand the language and those who have to wait for the interpreter and it's great if you get it right and there's a second wave of laughter, but sometimes you know it's impossible and the only thing you can do is say 'the speaker is telling a joke but I'm afraid I don't understand it: please laugh when I ask you to'. If you're taking your audience with you they usually do.

Man: Poetry's another one. If someone starts quoting verse you get completely lost. But overall I don't think it's the content that matters so much as the delivery; many speakers can write well but are quite incapable of expressing themselves verbally, yet we somehow turn it into a smooth flow of coherent speech.

Woman 2: Yeah, some of them drive you up the wall. I mean often they use prepared texts and might not even have read it through – all they're interested in is seeing it in the minutes and it comes out . . . it comes out as complete rubbish.

Woman 1: Or they stutter, they've got speech impediments or loose false teeth, or their performance is just downright neurotic.

Woman 2: But it's when one of them says 'I'm sorry, but the interpreter's made a mistake' when he's gone too far and somebody else has jumped up to protest – you look at your colleagues and you know that you haven't but there's this guy insisting 'I never said that' and you feel like walking out.

Man: These are usually diplomatic incidents and you're supposed to accept this, and smile and apologize; but nowadays interpreters are less willing to do so and on occasions break in to explain. The speakers just can't believe it when the machine talks back to them.

Woman 1: Right. And most of the time you do feel as though you're doing a little bit to help international communication.

Woman 2: But I get the feeling when it's all over – a kind of flatness – when I think about the sound quality, the speakers, the working conditions and I find myself wondering 'Why couldn't we have made a better job of it?'.

Man: Oh, I don't know. It makes it a challenge: you've got to anticipate all the time and it's not often boring is it? And when you do get it right you feel great.

Now listen to the piece again.

TEST ONE: Fourth part

*You will hear a financial news report. Look at questions **17–19**. For questions **17** and **18**, fill in the currency rates in the spaces provided. For question **19** tick the appropriate boxes. You will hear the piece twice.*

. . . In Tokyo, the dollar closed firmer, but with gains limited by intervention. The dollar finished in Tokyo at 143,335 yen, 1.9655 marks, and against sterling at 1 dollar 56.15 cents. The pound is steady but vulnerable, until the release of the latest UK current account figures on Wednesday.

Now the latest currency rates in London: the pound is 25 points weaker than Friday's London close, at one dollar 56.8 cents. The sterling index is up point 3 at 91.3; the German mark down 35 points at 1 mark 96.25. The swiss franc down 50 points at 1 franc 69.15; the French franc down 140 points at 6 francs 61.55. But the Japanese yen, up 10 points at 142.8. The Dutch guilder, down 75 points at 2 guilders 21.25; the Australian dollar in Sydney closed point 15 cents higher at 75.8 US cents. And the American long bond ended firmer in Tokyo. Closing up . . .

Now listen to the piece again.

TEST TWO: First part

*You will hear a radio phone-in on the subject of nuclear energy. Look at questions **1–6**. For each qustion tick one of the boxes **A**, **B**, **C** or **D**. You will hear the piece twice.*

Interviewer: Tonight I've got with me in the studio Edward Hall of the Energy Authority, and he's going to answer your questions . . . I hope.
Hall: Well, I'll try to do my best.
Interviewer: Right . . . now there's a caller on line 1 . . . hello who's speaking please and what is your question?
Caller: John Stokes from Cumbria and what I'd like to know is how anyone can seriously say they're in favour of nuclear power after Chernobyl, Sellafield, Three Mile Island and things like that? What's it going to take to make you people realise that the risks are just too big?
Hall: Well the first thing I'd like to say is that Chernobyl – the only civilian nuclear accident ever to kill anyone – was caused by an unsafe reactor of a type that would never be allowed in this country or in places like France for that matter where nearly 75% of electricity generation is nuclear. Nuclear power is safer and cleaner than any other substantial and practicable source of electricity. You only have to look at the question of waste. For nuclear power, a little bit of uranium is dug up, refined, put through a reactor, stored and then put back into the ground. This waste is dangerous at first, but its shorter half-life means that over the long term it's safer than the original uranium in the ground that it comes from, as this gives off radon, the radioactive gas now known to cause cancer. And don't forget that the greenhouse effect and acid rain are being brought about by fossil fuel burning, not nuclear power stations. And furthermore . . .
Interviewer: Are you satisfied with that answer, Mr Stokes?
Caller: No I certainly am not. To say that there's only ever been one fatal nuclear accident is just to take part in the massive cover-up that's gone on for decades now, and to dismiss Chernobyl as a one-off mistake that couldn't happen here shows total ignorance, to be charitable, of the effects throughout Europe and beyond, as well as callous disregard for those who died and the 1,600 who will die – World Health Organisation figures – let alone . . .
Hall: I do . . . I really do feel as sad as anyone about the effects of that horrific tragedy, but I've also seen at first hand the effects of coal pollution on people, and I'm afraid, Mr Stokes, that the evidence shows that the radiation, in the form of cadmium, and the chemicals which are released into the atmosphere by coal burning are far more devastating: now a recent study puts the number of deaths per year in the US at over 25,000. Then there's the question of danger in the actual mining process: did you know that coal mining kills more than ten times as many . . .
Caller: Well I'm sure your figures are right, but why are we talking just about coal? What about all those so-called alternative ways of producing energy – you know: tides and waves, the wind and all the rest we've been hearing about for so long? When are they actually going to happen and how are you people going to make sure they do?
Hall: Well you must bear in mind the fact that the contribution to the country's total power needs of all those 'renewable' sources will never even reach five per cent.
Caller: How can you possibly be so certain of that? And what if we drastically reduce overall energy consumption? Which brings me on to another point . . .

Now listen to the piece again.

TEST TWO: Second part

*You will hear an extract from a programme in which homeless teenagers in London are interviewed. Look at question **7**. For each person write the number of the comment in the boxes provided. You will hear the piece twice.*

Presenter: On these wet and cold December evenings we've been out talking to some of the 50,000 young people who sleep rough every night on the streets of London. The first person we spoke to was Julie, who's just 16. After the death of her mother last year her dad simply walked out:

Julie: I want him to see this interview, to see my picture. He might come back if he sees what's happened to me.

Presenter: She held up a picture of herself taken two years ago. Her blonde hair is short and smart, eyes strongly mascaraed, skin clear.

Julie: See what's become of me?

Presenter: Her boyfriend Paul is nearly 18 and has come down from Liverpool in search of work:

Paul: I just couldn't stand hanging around up there all day just sitting there watching TV. There is just no work at all up there. I had to get out and look for a job.

Presenter: Sitting next to them was Tony, who had been in care since the age of nine:

Tony: I'm angry about what's happened to me. I'm very angry. When I came out of care they said they would find me somewhere to live – but they just forgot about me.

Presenter: Next we spoke to Sharon, who's just 17 and says she left home because she had a row with her mum. We asked her if she'd tried to join a Youth Training Scheme:

Sharon: Of course I have. But they told me I had to give my home address and I didn't have one. Anyway you can't go into work after sleeping on the streets, can you? You just can't do it. It's embarrassing, you feel so awful.

Presenter: Sean is a skinhead with 'made in England' tattooed across his neck:

Sean: I can get you younger kids, I could even get you one girl who has her own kid.

Presenter: As we walked back across the bridge Paul looked down at the waters of the Thames and said to himself:

Paul: I wish it was the Mersey down there.

Now listen to the piece again.

TEST TWO: Third part

*You will hear a review of a book about aliens visiting Earth. Look at questions **8–12**. For each question tick one of the boxes **A**, **B**, **C** or **D**. You will hear the piece twice.*

Presenter: Today in *New Books* we look at 'Above top secret: the worldwide UFO cover-up'.

Reviewer: I don't know how many trees were cut down to produce this 590-page diatribe, but I wish they had been left standing. It is an evil book. Little of it is original, much of it is false. The implications seem to recommend a witch hunt. The central thesis is that thousands of alien spacecraft, filled with alien beings, regularly visit the Earth. And the reason we know nothing about them is that there is a vast inter-governmental conspiracy to keep their existence secret.

Now there are two good reasons why this is extremely improbable, and this book does not mention either of them. Any spaceship capable of crossing the vast gulfs between the stars, even if it only carried a dozen crewmen, would have to weigh more than 50,000 tons. It would be as big as a supertanker. It would need this mass and volume to accommodate both its engines and its immense quantities of fuel.

For the distances between the stars are on average a million times greater than those between our local planets. Mars, at its closest approach, is a 'mere' 49 million miles away. But the distance to the nearest star, Proxima Centauri, is a staggering 26 *million million* miles. A ship that could cover that distance within a reasonable voyage time would need stupendous capabilities of acceleration and deceleration. It would be a vehicle of truly monstrous power and size. It no way could its dimensions be shrunk, as the author glibly assumes, to the size of an executive jet.

Nor, if it landed on Earth, could it be concealed by any terrestrial government. It would be equally impossible for it to remain secretly in Earth's orbit while its scoutships descended to the surface. It would be spotted within hours by observers in Jodrell Bank and Norad – not to mention any competent amateur with binoculars. And it does not occur to the writer that the creatures who would undertake such a voyage would be very much cleverer than we are. It is ridiculous to suggest that our government officials, with their puny technology, would be able to arrest them or kill them off.

This book shows no signs of the author being aware of the progress in space science, or even in terrestrial exploration, that has been made in the last two decades. 'I have been informed by reliable sources,' he writes, 'that some of them (the aliens) have bases within the solar system, or even here on Earth.' How strange then, that Nasa's unmanned space probes, which have scoured the solar system, and the explorers who have examined every part of our own planet's surface, have found no trace of such 'bases'.

I have called this book 'evil' and I mean it. The ideas are those of a maniac. But it is written with a certain coarse eloquence, and there is a danger that others as uneducated as the author might be infected.

Now listen to the piece again.   ***Adrian Berry**. Science Correspondent of The Daily Telegraph*

TEST TWO: Fourth part

You will hear a parent trying to describe young people's speech. Look at question 13. Tick whether you think the statements are true or false. You will hear the piece twice.

Even the best TV programmes for kids have a major fault: they are more or less comprehensible. The paradox about teenage dialogue is that if you can understand it, it's not authentic. The adult viewer loses out either way. If he can understand what the kids are saying, he's being fobbed off with bogus material; and if he can't understand it, then he can't understand it, and might as well watch Saudi Arabian TV on his satellite dish.

I do not understand my children. I do not understand what they say, and not just what they say but the way in which they say it. This is intentional. Just as parents used to drop into French in order to fool their offspring and servants, so children now scramble their private conversations into their own vernacular. It's about time a scriptwriter came up with an entire series in 'Childspeak'. It would need subtitles, but so do most Channel 4 movies and no one complains.

'G-language' is nationwide and therefore suitable for a networked programme. It is perfectly simple, at least when compared with Mandarin Chinese or the trickier Urdu dialects. Take, for example, the expression 'Relaguth is a fish'. This is nothing to do with aquaria. 'Fish' is not G-language, but an insult; it means, as the accompanying body language will immediately suggest, 'stupid'. Those not fluent in Childspeak would never guess, but 'Relaguth' is 'Ruth': this is obtained by pronouncing the first letter phonetically, then adding an 'l-g' and finally, the remainder of the syllable. It helps to start a Teach Yourself G-language course with mono-syllabic words, since every syllable of every word in English ends up as three in G-language. In other words, my children think their mother, Ruth, is not Mensa material. No wonder kids talk all the time; they have to speak three times as fast just to keep up with parents.

My children are bilingual. They can slip out of G-talk into what they call 'backslang', which involves taking the first letter of a word and shifting it to the back, before adding the letter 'a' – the sort of thing my word processor does all the time – so that my own Christian name becomes Onathanj and then Onathanja.

In its way more puzzling is a language which at first hearing appears to be our lingua franca and at second earful, turns out to emanate from aliens. Even a 'fish' like me has tumbled to the fact that 'bad' and 'wicked' both mean exactly the opposite, but I had no idea that other synonyms for 'good' include 'blinding', 'sweet' and – this is skate-talk – 'rad'. 'Safe' and 'crucial' are, to those in the know, another way of saying 'very good', while 'boomy' is what we wrinklies understand as 'brilliant'. So is 'the don'. Without being tipped off by some streetwise kid you would never work that one out, nor would you deduce that 'grommet' or 'grom' meant an 'eight-year-old skater kitted out with everything except skill'. 'Moshing' is Heavy Metal for 'headbanging'. If you have to ask for a definition of headbanging, or indeed Heavy Metal, that's your 'sike' – tough luck.

Your tired brains will appreciate something closer to the Queen's English. I'm not referring to gay talk but to expressions which are within striking distance of Parentspeak. 'Lipsing-up' is a somewhat poetic term for 'kissing' and 'caned' for 'canned' i.e. 'drunk'. You don't have to be a second Dr Johnson to work out that 'ped' started life as 'pedestrian'. But how 'shemeg' came to mean sex, 'renk' rude, 'coco' bruise and 'gathers' police, I have to leave to the more 'boffin' – clever, hardworking, of course – among you.

Now listen to the piece again.

TEST THREE: First part

You will hear a sports announcer talking about the round-the-world yacht race. Fill in the missing information, questions 1–9 in the spaces provided. You will hear the piece twice.

Years of planning, building and training, and millions of pounds of investment will reach the moment of truth in the Solent on the 2nd of September shortly after midday.

Nearly 400 competitors from fourteen countries on twenty four yachts ranging in size from 50 to 80 feet, will be setting off on the first 6281 miles of the round-the-world race. Over the following ten months or so they will navigate their way through the calm of the 'Doldrums', and roller coast through the 'Roaring Forties' on their 32,932 nautical mile voyage.

The first leg will take them south past the coast of West Africa and across the Atlantic to Punta del Este in Uruguay, arriving sometime between the 9th and the 18th of October. Choosing which side of the 'Doldrums' to go may mean stealing an early lead or being left far behind.

The destination for the 2nd and longest leg of the race will be Fremantle in Western Australia. On the 28th of October they will head off, helped along by the mighty gusts of the 'Roaring Forties', south of the Cape of Good Hope, aiming to arrive down under between the 29th of November and the 10th of December. The new race route avoids politically sensitive South Africa, instead incorporating Australia and New Zealand.

The much shorter third leg will start on the 23rd of December and will take them east, 3434 miles to the south of Tasmania following the flow of the depressions, to New Zealand, arriving in Aukland between the 12th and the 16th of January.

Continuing eastwards, the competitors will leave Auckland on the 4th of February for their return to Punta del Este. This longer stretch will take them across the Southern Ocean round Cape Horn and up the coast of South America to Uruguay. They will be helped along the 6255 mile fourth leg by prevailing westerly winds and are due to arrive in Uruguay between the 28th of February and the 8th of March.

By this time the crews will probably be very much in need of the customary few days break between each stretch of the race, before embarking on the fifth leg of their nearly 33,000 mile endurance test.

The 5th and penultimate leg will start on the 17th of March. The route will take them north, hugging the coast, past the eastern tip of Brazil, through the Caribbean and up to Fort Lauderdale in Miami, in the USA. The lack of wind off the north coast of Brazil is an obvious problem for any vessel under sail and this is the area known as 'The Doldrums'. Depending on the climatic activity here, the yachts are due to arrive in the United States between the 13th and the 21st of April. The crews will then have between two and three weeks to make the final preparations for the last push home.

The final leg of 3837 miles is expected to take the crews just 12 days or so. Departing from Fort Lauderdale on the 5th of May they will be helped along by the Gulf Stream which will carry them north-east towards Europe, arriving in The Solent between the 16th and the 23rd of May.

For some it will have been an expensive business promotion. Despite a costing of about $24,000 Australian to secure berths for the largest of the yachts, the sponsers see the race as an effective vehicle for spreading their particular message to new markets.

But for many others it will be the fulfilment of a dream as they battle with the elements and endure hardships in a personal 33,000 mile challenge.

Now listen to the piece again.

TEST THREE: Second part

*You will hear a report on pop records as collectors' items. Look at questions **10–14**. For each question tick one of the boxes **A**, **B**, **C** or **D**. You will hear the piece twice.*

The value of collectable pop records has more than doubled in the past five years. Elvis Presley's first three albums of 1956–57 can fetch about £100 each, while albums and singles sold over the counter as recently as 10 or 20 years ago are also fetching three-figure sums. Now is the time to search your hitherto unsellable collection for recordings by psychedelic groups of the late Sixties, progressives and funk of the early Seventies and punk/new wave of the late Seventies.

Original recordings by the three Bs – Bowie, Bolan and, at last, the Beatles – are booming. A dealer recently refused £2,000 for a copy of the 1963 album *Please Please Me*, the stereo version with gold and red label of which only about 200 were circulated. Three years ago, he reckons, it would have fetched £300–£400. Even the mono version changes hands for £100–£150.

The monthly *Record Collector*, at nearly 200 pages the fattest of the two enthusiasts' magazines, has upped its circulation from 30 thousand to 40 thousand in the past three years and 10-year-old copies of its earliest issues fetch £25. *Spiral Scratch*, launched to service the collectors' market for Seventies and Eighties recordings, hopes to double its 15,000 circulation when it starts national distribution next month.

As pressure of demand from collectors grows, the time it takes some records to double in value is shrinking from years to months. *Spiral Scratch*'s feature, Short Run, charts short-term price jumps like the going collectors' rate of £5–£6 for Madonna's single *Express Yourself* (with strategically placed zip on the cover) three months after it retailed for £1.99.

But the specialists have more confidence in older recordings. One lot of 11 singles on *Deram*, the short-lived label bravely launched in 1966 by Decca in pursuit of the illusive psychedelic market, went for £132. It included Bowie's low-circulation *Laughing Gnome* of 1967 which, re-released 10 years later in spite of his change of image, embarrassingly made the Top Ten. A copy of Marc Bolan's *The Third Degree* of 1966, which may have sold only 100 copies, made £198. And the Sex Pistols' 1977 punk single, *God Save the Queen* on the A & M label, is worth £500.

Now listen to the piece again.

TEST THREE: Third part

*You will hear some information on atmospheric phenomena for airline passengers. Look at questions **15–17**. For each of the questions tick one of the boxes **A**, **B**, **C** or **D**. You will hear the piece twice.*

... When you're flying at high altitude the sky is less polluted and therefore darker blue. From Concorde it's almost indigo blue. This is because of the scarcity of the minute, individually invisible airborne particles which scatter the light. On a polluted day at the Earth's surface there are billions of such tiny particles above us so even a cloud-free sky looks pale blue or almost milky white.

A large jet airliner flies at perhaps 38,000 feet where the air density is only 200 millibars compared with about 1,000 millibars at the surface. With the outside pressure well below that on the summit of Everest, humans wouldn't survive long and so the plane is pressurised – usually at 700 millibars, which is the equivalent of 10,000 feet.

People often return from holiday and ask meteorologists about strange cloud formations seen from the aircraft, often described as 'a long line of cloud ending quite abruptly'. It's usually impossible to give much explanation but three possibilities are suggested. First of all the cloud could be the leading edge of an approaching frontal system (or the rear edge of a departing one).

Second, a peninsula or island could be sheltering the area from a bank of low cloud or sea fog and the sudden edge marks the boundary between the sheltered area and exposed area. A third possibility is that a peninsula or island might be triggering convective (cumulus) cloud.

Tail winds may speed your journey and especially when you are travelling eastwards, since our jet-streams are mainly westerly.

Now listen to the piece again.

TEST THREE: Fourth part

*You will hear a news item about restrictions on TV and radio advertisements for charities. Look at question **18**. Tick the slogans which will be allowed under the code. You will hear the piece twice.*

Presenter: . . . The Independent Broadcasting Authority has today announced the setting up of a watchdog to ensure that advertisements for charities do not indulge in 'emotional overkill' and has laid down a seven-point code to guide advertisers. With me is Chris Williams, a member of the new committee. Chris, what will you be looking out for?

Williams: Well, apart from 'avoiding scripts of a political or religious nature' – so no propaganda or preaching, in other words – they must, to quote the code: 'handle with care and discretion any matters likely to arouse strong feelings'.

Presenter: They mustn't aim to shock, then, by using, say, close-ups of people who are suffering in any way.

Williams: That kind of thing, yes. The second point is that they 'must not indulge in emotional blackmail by suggesting that anyone lacks proper sympathy if they do not donate'. So no trying to make people feel guilty if they don't want to contribute. Next, all ads should 'respect the dignity of people who receive charity', 'not address fundraising messages to children', 'not compare themselves with other charities', 'not . . .

Presenter: That one means that you can't attack another charity by, for instance, implying that those who get help from it are showhow less deserving than the people you're helping, right?

Williams: That's the idea, yes. Now something else they mustn't do is 'give exaggerated, non-typical examples of the problem they are seeking to alleviate'.

Presenter: That's not going to be an easy one to pin down.

Williams: I know. But I think if the case that's used to dramatise the issue is the kind of thing that would make a good headline for the . . . the more sensationalist end of the press spectrum, then . . . then we'd probably be against it.

Presenter: There might be a few headlines against you tomorrow morning!

Williams: It wouldn't be first time. Now the final point: they must 'not mislead donors about how their money will be used'. Now, I don't think we'll have to deal here with many cases of actual deception – at least I hope not – I think it'll be more a question of over-optimism on the part of some charities. I reckon the safest thing here would probably be for the ads not to make any big claims at all, because circumstances can change for the worse almost overnight when you're dealing with, say, famine in war zones or . . . or epidemic relief or disasters like that . . . . so saying things like 'We'll feed Africa' would be very rash, to say the least.

Presenter: Thanks, Chris.

Williams: Thank you, Jane.

Now listen to the piece again.

TEST FOUR: First part

*You will hear a radio programme in which the subject of queueing is discussed. Look at question **1**. Tick whether you think the statements are true or false. You will hear the piece twice.*

Presenter: If you find yourself waiting in a long queue at an airport or bus terminus this holiday, will you try to analyse what it is about queueing that makes you angry? Or will you just vent your spleen on the nearest official?

Professor Richard Larson, an electrical engineer at the Massachusetts Institute of Technology, hates queueing, but rather than tear his hair out he decided to study the subject.

His first finding, which backed up earlier work at the US National Science Foundation, was that the degree of annoyance was not directly related to the time wasted.

Professor Larson, how did you come to this conclusion?

Larson: Well, there was an experiment at Houston airport where passengers had to walk for one minute from the plane to the baggage reclaim, and then wait a further seven minutes to collect their luggage. Complaints were frequent, especially from those who had spent seven minutes watching passengers with just hand baggage get out immediately. Anyhow, the airport authorities decided to lengthen the walk from the aircraft, so that instead of a one-minute trot, the passengers spent six minutes walking. When they finally arrived at the baggage reclaim, the delay was then only two minutes. The extra walk extended the delay – by five minutes for those carrying only hand baggage – but passenger complaints dropped almost to zero.

Presenter: How do you account for that?

Larson: I believe it all has to do with social justice. If people see others taking a short cut, they find the wait unbearable. So in the case of the airport, it was preferable to delay everyone.

Presenter: What else has come to light during your research?

Larson: Something else we observed was the fact that people get more fed up if they are not told what is going on. Passengers told that there will be a half-hour delay are less unhappy than those left waiting even 20 minutes without an explanation. But even knowing how long we have to wait isn't the whole answer. We must also believe that everything is being done to minimise our delay.

Presenter: Can you give us an example of that?

Larson: Sure. We looked at two neighbouring American banks. One was highly computerised and served a customer, on average, every 30 seconds. The other bank was less automated and took twice as long. But because the tellers at the second bank looked frantically busy, customers believed the service was faster and many transferred their accounts to the slower bank. Ultimately, the first one had to introduce time-wasting ways of appearing more dynamic.

Presenter: Professor Larson, thank you very much.

Larson: You're welcome.

Now listen to the piece again.

TEST FOUR: Second part

You will hear about sunken treasure in the seas of South East Asia. For question 2 you should fill in the missing information. You will hear the piece twice.

Storms, currents, reefs and rivalry between powers left these waters littered with sunken wrecks and it's only recently that the Indonesian Government has realised what it's sitting on.

For example, there's the British frigate *Alcieste* which sank in 1817 and was said to be carrying gold; the *Intrepid*, an American tea clipper which went down in 1860 could be carrying Nanking porcelain; and the *Lindenhoff*, a Dutch ship which foundered in 1765 with a cargo of tin and silver.

But what really alerted the authorities was Michael Hatcher's treasure-hunting. In 1985 he was looking for the *Geldermalsen*, a ship of the Dutch East India company reputed to have been carrying gold, porcelain and silk when she went down in 1752. The first wreck he found was not the big 'G', but a seventeenth century Chinese junk carrying $3 million worth of Ming porcelain. The *Geldermalsen* turned up later: it contained chest after chest of perfect porcelain which was auctioned in Amsterdam. Hatcher walked off with $15 million.

Both government ministers and archaeologists are keen to avoid the same fate befalling the contents of the *Flor de la Mar*, which sank on a sandbank in 1511. It is said to be the richest wreck in the world – Portuguese records say she had just taken the vital trading port of Malacca and was returning home laden with gold and precious stones which could be worth up to $8 billion.

Now listen to the piece again.

TEST FOUR: Third part

You will hear a radio programme about mobile telephones. Look at questions 3–5. For questions 3 and 5 tick one of the boxes A, B, C or D. For question 4 tick the things which the phone users complain about in the boxes provided. You will hear the piece twice.

Presenter: Once the mobile phone was the ultimate portable pose, the device no self-respecting Porsche driver would be seen in public without. But that was before 'cellular fatigue'. Four years into the telecommunications revolution, the wealthy are finding that clinching deals in a traffic jam, or buying shares while out sailing, may not represent the biggest freedom on earth. For many the constant bleeping or vibrating – there are now phones that shudder rather than ring – has become purgatory. Martin Olley has a company in London and commutes from Kent:

Olley: I just want to meditate, to mull over things in life. But there's always someone after me. Of a dozen calls, one might be crucial for business. But I'm just going to switch off and get rid of the phone and I am not going to worry about the consequences.

Presenter: Even people in the mobile phone business are not immune. Gary Parker, managing director of Roadphones:

Parker: I spend most car journeys permanently engaged. I tried changing numbers but it didn't work. You're always pestered. I know I tell customers that the advantage of the telephone is that you can switch it off, but if you do that you worry you are losing business. Not any more – I've had enough.

Presenter: According to Peter Bruggen, a psychiatrist who offers counselling to businessmen, many people feel persecuted by their phones:

Bruggen: The stress builds up when a person's relationship to all this talk is such that he feels the slave rather than the master. He may complain of backache, headache, tenseness – all the symptoms of badly-handled stress.

Presenter: But the big mobile telephone dealers claim not to have heard of cellular fatigue. A spokesman said:

Spokesman: You'd have to be pretty unimaginative to suffer from it. You can always turn the phone off or divert the call. There are very few reasons why people give up phones by choice, and 'cellular fatigue' isn't one of 'em. It's normally if they have moved away, changed jobs, can't afford the calls, or go to prison.

Now listen to the piece again.

TEST FOUR: Fourth part

You will hear an interview with a mixed-nationality couple. Look at questions 6–8. For each question tick one of the boxes A, B, C or D. You will hear the piece twice.

Kevin: Well I think the first myth is that you kind of learn your partner's language without even trying to – by osmosis or something – when in fact what happens is that when you are used to speaking to someone in a certain language it seems weird somehow to change to another; and Marian's English was so good that there was never any question about which one we'd use.

Marian: And anyway it'd be like teaching your boyfriend to drive.

Kevin: On the wrong side of the road, of course.

Marian: Naturally.

Interviewer: How do you cope with the huge range of cultural differences?

Marian: There's some that don't matter at all really, but when you're talking about essentials you've got to reach some sort of compromise, like our agreement on food and mealtimes: as much variety as possible and late eating in summer, early in winter.

Interviewer: And spring and autumn?

Kevin: Arguments about whether it's hot or cold usually – sometimes it's stifling in here but she wants the heating on . . .

Marian: He's always flinging the windows open when it's freezing and everyone's sitting here shivering and sneezing . . .

Interviewer: I suppose, though, that you don't have to be from different countries to disagree about things like the ideal temperature?

Kevin: Yeah, the truth is that you tend to make more allowances for different attitudes to things – you think, well, we've grown up in different worlds and you've got to remember that. You're probably more understanding than you would be with someone from your own country who's from a different background.

Marian: That's all very well but sometimes it sounds to me like a cross-cultural con – you're supposed to 'make allowances' for things that don't exist anywhere outside his imagination . . .

Kevin: Such as?

Marian: Such as when you told me that 'everyone back home' was out till 12 every night with his mates, and then I spoke to a few women who came from the same place, and there's the little matter of your drinking . . .

Kevin: Do you have to . . .

Marian: I'm just keeping to the cultural aspects Kev: you said the local booze is undrinkable but you get through enough of it . . .

Kevin: At least I don't drink during the day.

Marian: At least *we* manage to stay sober.

Kevin: Don't you mean *they*? Since you've been living with me you've learnt how to drink.

Marian: And I thought that with you I was going to learn . . .

Kevin: Oh come on, you know that what we've got in common cuts right across cultural barriers.

Marian: You mean music – yes well that does help. When you share something like that things tend to work out a bit easier.

Interviewer: Would you say that's the best aspect of your relationship?

Kevin: Yeah – that and the fact that when your partner's from another culture you're never bored.

Marian: Well, not often anyway . . .

Now listen to the piece again.

ANSWER KEY

TEST ONE

Paper 1 — Reading Comprehension

Section A – one mark for each correct answer.

| 1 C | 2 A | 3 D | 4 C | 5 B | 6 C | 7 A | 8 D | 9 C | 10 C | 11 A | 12 C |
| 13 B | 14 B | 15 C | 16 D | 17 D | 18 D | 19 B | 20 C | 21 B | 22 D | 23 B | 24 C |
| 25 A |

Total: 25

Section B – two marks for each correct answer.

| 26 D | 27 C | 28 B | 29 A | 30 C | 31 B | 32 B | 33 D | 34 B | 35 A | 36 B | 37 D |
| 38 A | 39 D | 40 B |

Total: 30

Paper 3 — Use of English

Section A

Question 1 – one mark for each correct answer.
1 psychological/mental **2** tend **3** to **4** from **5** over **6** lead **7** in **8** back **9** each/either **10** wrong/up **11** no **12** straight **13** as **14** another **15** into **16** forward **17** treatment/attention/care **18** hand **19** to/of **20** aware/conscious.

Total: 20

Question 2 – one mark for each word or phrase between the vertical lines. Ignore the words printed in *italics*.
a *Is* | there any point in going | *to the meeting.* (1 mark)
b *Brilliant* | though/as he was, | *he never became famous.* (1 mark)
c *Nowhere* | else in the world will | you see | *cliffs like these.* (2 marks)
d *However* | long it takes, the jobs's | *got to be finished.* (1 mark)
　　　　　 | long the job takes, it's |
e *It is not yet clear* | why there is/was etc. a delay. |
　　　　　　　　　 | what the reasons for the delay are. | (1 mark)
f *Not* | knowing what to do next | *he rang me up.* (1 mark)
g *Not a* | single crew member | survived | *the explosion.* (2 marks)
h *To his* | intense | annoyance | *the car wouldn't start.* (2 marks)

Total: 11

Question 3 – one mark for each word or phrase between the vertical lines. Ignore the words printed in *italics*.
a *They look identical! How can you* | tell which (one) | *is which?* (1 mark)
b *It won't be long* | before/until he gets/he's | *fed up with that job.* (1 mark)
c *Should* | you need/want | *any help, just call me.* (1 mark)
d *Has it ever* | occurred to you | *that you might be wasting your time?* (1 mark)
　　　　　 | crossed your mind |
e *We had a lovely holiday, but on* | returning/coming back etc | *we found*
　　　　　　　　　　　　　 | our return |
the house had been burgled. (1 mark)
f *It really is time he retired. By June he* | will have been | *working there for 40 years.* (1 mark)

Total: 6

Question 4 – one mark for each word or phrase between the vertical lines. Ignore the words printed in *italics*.
a | I am not prepared to pay him. | (1 mark)
b *He got to the meeting* | with two minutes | to spare. | (2 marks)
c | We have our misgivings | *about your plans.* (1 mark)
d | Would you like (me to give you) a lift | *to the airport?* (1 mark)
　　 | Could I give you a lift |
e | He does nothing | but sleep | *all day.* (2 marks)
　　 | He doesn't do anything |
f *When the sun went down* | there was a | sharp fall | in (the) temperature. | (3 marks)
g | There is a ban on demonstrations | *outside the palace.* (1 mark)
h *The Minister* | has given the project the go-ahead. |
　　　　　　　 | has given the go-ahead to the project. | (1 mark)

Total: 12

Section B
Question 5 – the mark shown for each question for coherent and relevant answers, not necessarily echoing the wording given here.

a It refers to the nature of the terrain through which the road ran.   (1)
b Antagonistic religious groups (1) were shooting at each other from either side of the valley (1).
c He went somewhere he couldn't be overheard (1) to practise an expression in the driver's language (1).
d to warn of excessive speed   (1)
e a very tight bend   (1)
f collide   (1)
g because he had told Azad to slow down (1) and so they had got there after dinner-time (1)
h because he thinks '20th-century miracle' is an exaggeration   (1)
i to link China with Pakistan (and India)   (1)
j There are lorry convoys only once a year (1) and the local people are too poor to own vehicles (1).
k turbulent, fast-moving and bubbling etc.   (1)
l unmade roads (1) with trees alongside (1)
m because they ignored the special water (1) and did not stay with the local people (1)
n unimportant – unless the cracked lens covered his good eye (1); that it made the journey even more hazardous (1)
o One mark each for inclusion of the following eight points, plus an impression mark of 0–4 for a well-expressed, cohesive paragraph, penalising irrelevance, indiscriminate lifting and subjective comment:
— warring religious factions
— rocks falling on the road
— animals on the road
— crazy lorry drivers
— few safety barriers
— tight bends
— distracting views
— one-eyed driver
Total: 33

Paper 4 — Listening Comprehension

1st part: **1** C   **2** B   **3** A   **4** D   **5** A   **6** D
Total: 6
2nd part: **7** A   **8** C   **9** C   **10** A
Total: 4
3rd part: **11** D   **12** A   **13** B   **14** D   **15** B   **16** D
Total: 6
4th part: **17** 143.335   **18** 1$ 56.15 cents (1 mark each)   **19 a** fall **b** fall **c** rise **d** rise
($\frac{1}{2}$ mark each)

Total: 4

TEST TWO

Paper 1 — Reading Comprehension

Section A – one mark for each correct answer.

1 A   **2** B   **3** C   **4** A   **5** C   **6** D   **7** B   **8** A   **9** C   **10** C   **11** A   **12** D
13 C   **14** C   **15** B   **16** D   **17** A   **18** B   **19** C   **20** A   **21** C   **22** D   **23** B   **24** C
25 B
Total: 25

Section B – two marks for each correct answer.
26 C   **27** D   **28** B   **29** D   **30** B   **31** A   **32** B   **33** B   **34** A   **35** D   **36** B   **37** B
38 A   **39** C   **40** A
Total: 30

Paper 3 — Use of English

Section A
Question 1 – one mark for each correct answer.
1 goes/dates **2** As/While/When **3** the **4** spending **5** then **6** them **7** of **8** which **9** To/For **10** those/matters etc. **11** away **12** which **13** was **14** are **15** where **16** of **17** brought/created etc. **18** world **19** rarer **20** in
Total: 20

Question 2 – one mark for each word or phrase between the vertical lines. Ignore the words printed in *italics*.
a *What's wrong* | with leaving | *the hardest part till tomorrow?* (1 mark)
b *Besides* | being hot | it's also sunny | *in Greece at this time of the year.* (2 marks)
c *It was* | very brave of him | to refuse | *to obey the order.* (2 marks)
d *What worries them is not* | so much the workload | as the initial outlay. | (2 marks)
e *Rarely* | is a performance of such quality seen anywhere. | (1 mark)
f *Their* | constant | encouragement | *made her job easier.* (2 marks)
g *I was* | rather puzzled by | *their reaction.* (1 mark)
h *Not* | for a second did she let them | *out of her sight* (1 mark)
Total: 12

Question 3 – one mark for each word or phrase between the vertical lines. Ignore the words printed in *italics*.
a *This is the second time this week (that) you* | have arrived/got here etc. | *late.* (1 mark)
b *You* | didn't need to take | *a taxi. The bus came a few seconds later.* (1 mark)
          | needn't have taken |
c *Never in the history of science* | was there | *such a breakthrough.* (1 mark)
                                        | has there been |
d *I didn't want to go to the party anyway. I'd sooner* | have stayed | *at home and watched TV.* (1 mark)
e *I'm sorry for* | not letting you | *know before, but I couldn't contact you.* (1 mark)
                      | not having let you |
f *If only* | I hadn't lost | *my temper with her. We'd still be together now.* (1 mark)
Total: 6

Question 4 – one mark for each word or phrase between the vertical lines. Ignore the words printed *in italics*.
a *This Government* | has sought the elimination of poverty. |
                        | has sought to eliminate poverty. |
     | The elimination of poverty has been sought by | *this Government.* (1 mark)
b *They made* | an utter/a complete/an absolute (etc) | fool | of him. |
                  | him look (like) | an utter/a complete/an absolute (etc) | fool. | (2 marks)
c *The President did not* | rule out | *further measures.* (1 mark)
d *I'll* | have a word with him. | (1 mark)
e | What's the score in the cup final? |
      | What's the cup final score? | (1 mark)
f *She* | has a | deep mistrust | *of anything new.*
     Her reaction to | anything new | is one of deep mistrust. | (2 marks)
g *We have* | made all | the arrangements | *for your stay.* (2 marks)
h *They were* | under constant | attack | *from all directions.* (2 marks)
Total: 12

Section B
Question 5 – the mark shown for each question for coherent and relevant answers, not necessarily echoing the wording given here.
a played their music (1) violently (1)
b bands that failed (1) and those that have no future (1)
c Peel's loyal supporters (1) and a few cases of the rock business actually promoting good groups (1)
d It was postponed (1) because of difficulties with contracts (1).
e from the early Seventies until about a year ago (1)
f pirate/illegally copied (1)
g *Strange Fruit Records* (1)
h something not expressed strongly enough (1)
i not thinking about the future results of what is done now (1)
j Some have been erased (1) and others stolen (1) by people who may or may not have worked for the BBC (1).
k when records come out (1)
l by including the known and the old (1); the modern and the unknown (1)

m a permanent account of events (1)
n it would not make bands sound better than they really are (1)
o One mark each for inclusion of the following nine points, plus an impression mark of 0–4 for a well-expressed, cohesive paragraph, penalising irrelevance, indiscriminate lifting and subjective comment:

(reasons) — pirate copies being made
             — Peel wanted groups to be paid
             — range and quality of music on Peel programme over 2 decades
(steps) — decide which recordings to use
             — if possible, get them from the BBC
             — get clearance from the band's record company
             — decide when each album will come out
             — vary the kinds of music
             — pay the BBC for the original recordings (13)

Total: 34

Paper 4 — Listening Comprehension

1st part: **1** B **2** C **3** A **4** C **5** B **6** B
          Total: 6
2nd part: **7** Julie 6 Sharon 8 Paul 5 Sean 4 Tony 2
          Total: 5
3rd part: **8** D **9** D **10** D **11** A **12** D
          Total: 5
4th part: **13 a** False **b** False **c** True **d** False **e** True **f** False **g** True
          h True ($\frac{1}{2}$ mark each)
          Total: 4

TEST THREE

Paper 1 — Reading Comprehension

Section A – one mark for each correct answer.
1 D **2** D **3** B **4** C **5** A **6** B **7** B **8** C **9** C **10** B **11** B **12** D
13 D **14** D **15** A **16** D **17** B **18** C **19** C **20** C **21** C **22** A **23** A **24** B
25 C
Total: 25

Section B – two marks for each correct answer.
26 B **27** D **28** B **29** D **30** C **31** C **32** D **33** A **34** A **35** D **36** B **37** B
38 D **39** B **40** A
Total: 30

Paper 3 — Use of English

Section A
Question 1 – one mark for each correct answer.
1 even/just/simply/maybe/perhaps **2** on **3** have **4** direction **5** one **6** let/see **7** into **8** life
9 prefer **10** on **11** design/plan **12** in **13** getting **14** rather **15** about **16** Crime **17** long
18 many **19** in **20** against/on
Total: 20

Question 2 – one mark for each word or phrase between the vertical lines. Ignore the words printed in *italics*.
a *Not* | being able to move | *it himself, he asked for help.* (1 mark)
       | being capable of moving |
b *Working* | night shifts is something | (that) I would really hate to have to do. | (2 marks)
c *His* | every move was being observed. | (1 mark)
d *Talking* | about it took us more time | *than actually doing it.* (1 mark)
e *At no* | stage of the process | is there | any | *risk of contamination.* (3 marks)
f *The management* | has not reinstated any | *of the sacked workers.* (1 mark)
                  | has refused to reinstate any |
g *Failure* | to pay | will result in/lead to etc. | your being | *prosecuted.* (3 marks)
h *What* | was most amazing | about the crime | *was its sheer audacity.* (2 marks)
Total: 14

Question 3 – one mark for each word or phrase between the vertical lines. Ignore the words printed in *italics*.
a *In no way* | are/were you etc. to | *blame for what happened.* (1 mark)
            | is/was he etc to |
b *She* | can't be/have got etc | *back yet or she'd have phoned by now.* (1 mark)
c *Had his brakes been working properly* | he wouldn't/mightn't have | *crashed.* (1 mark)

d *The dining room looks so much better since you* | did/tidied it | *up.* (1 mark)
e *They don't stand* | a/any/the slightest etc. chance of | *beating us in the final.* (1 mark)
f *At his age he* | should/ought to know | *better than to behave like that.* (1 mark)
Total: 6

Question 4 – one mark for each word or phrase between the vertical lines. Ignore the words printed in *italics*.
a | Fancy seeing | *her there!* (1 mark)
b *Why do you* | make | such a fuss | *about such trivial incidents?* (2 marks)
c *They can't afford the deposit,* | let alone | *the instalments.* (1 mark)
d | He's the | spitting image of | *that man on television.* (2 marks)
e *Do* | drop me a line | *when you get there.* (1 mark)
f *Her reaction* | came as | no real surprise. | (2 marks)
g *The outbreak* | was confined to | *a relatively small area.* (1 mark)
h *Please reply* | by return (of post). | (1 mark)
Total: 11

Section B
Question 5 – the mark shown for each question for coherent and relevant answers, not necessarily echoing the wording given here.
a in their natural habitat   (1)
b fifteen years   (1)
c If not, we would have the false impression (1) that chimpanzees' behaviour is peaceful (1).
d an urge to hurt others   (1)
e She now saw them as less predictable (1), more violent (1) and more than ever like human beings (1).
f to show they use tools (1), which made the criterion used to distinguish between humans and apes redundant (1)
g they know what they look like (1), they use tools (1) and a sophisticated form of communication (1)
h When something is put on a chimpanzee's face (1) he will know it is his image in the mirror (1) and remove what has been placed there (1).
i It is possible that we will regard them as even more like ourselves.   (1)
j started wiping out   (1)
k They had become different from each other with the passing of time (1) and chimpanzees dislike 'strangers' (1).
l looking for trouble by going near other groups' areas   (1)
m Before any of the others from their community (1), they went towards other groups when they heard their voices (1) and stayed longer when there was the chance of violence (1).
n mindlessly violent (1); to compare their behaviour with aggressive urban youths (1)
o One mark each for inclusion of the following seven points, plus an impression mark of 0–4 for a well-expressed, cohesive paragraph, penalising irrelevance, indiscriminate lifting and subjective comment:
— organised attacks on others of the same species
— the use of tools
— conscious of what they look like
— highly-developed oral communication
— killing off enemy groups
— young males' enjoyment of taking risks
— some waiting for trouble to start   (11)
Total: 37

Paper 4 — Listening Comprehension

1st part: **1** 2 Sept ($\frac{1}{2}$ mark)   **2** 6281 (1 mark)   **3** Roaring Forties (1 mark)   **4** 29 Nov ($\frac{1}{2}$ mark) — 10 Dec ($\frac{1}{2}$ mark)   **5** 4 Feb ($\frac{1}{2}$ mark)   **6** 6255 (1 mark)   **7** Doldrums (1 mark)   **8** Gulf Stream (1 mark)   **9** 16 May ($\frac{1}{2}$ mark) — 23 May ($\frac{1}{2}$ mark)
    Total: 8
2nd part: **10** A   **11** A   **12** C   **13** B   **14** D
    Total: 5
3rd part: **15** C   **16** B   **17** B
    Total: 3
4th part: **18 a**   **b**√   **c**   **d**√   **e**   **f**   **g**   **h**√   ($\frac{1}{2}$ mark for each correctly ticked or left blank)
    Total: 4

TEST FOUR

Paper 1 — Reading Comprehension

Section A – one mark for each correct answer.

1 A	**2** C	**3** A	**4** D	**5** B	**6** B	**7** D	**8** C	**9** B	**10** B	**11** D	**12** B
13 D	**14** A	**15** B	**16** C	**17** A	**18** D	**19** A	**20** B	**21** B	**22** C	**23** C	**24** D
25 A											

Total: 25

Section B – two marks for each correct answer.

26 C	**27** D	**28** D	**29** B	**30** A	**31** A	**32** C	**33** D	**34** C	**35** A	**36** D	**37** D
38 C	**39** B	**40** C									

Total: 30

Paper 3 — Use of English

Section A

Question 1 – one mark for each correct answer.
1 replace/substitute **2** used **3** on/with **4** up/out **5** an **6** according **7** makes **8** own **9** to **10** For **11** known **12** free **13** like **14** up **15** without **16** everyone **17** association/group/organisation **18** Imagine **19** started/began **20** on
Total: 20

Question 2 – one mark for each word or phrase between the vertical lines. Ignore the words printed in *italics*.
a *He was out* | of his depth. | (1 mark)
b *She found* | the demanding timetable quite exhausting. | (1 mark)
c *With the* | exception of | *Alain Prost* | no-one/nobody | *has won more Formula One races.*
(2 marks)
d *Despite* | having little in common they | *still get on very well together.* (1 mark)
    | the fact (that) they have little in common they |
e *The company made* | a substantial loss | *last year.* (1 mark)
f *It is* | doubtful whether | there will be | *an early announcement.* (2 marks)
g *He claimed that more* | was being spent | *on education than ever before.* (1 mark)
h *Apart* | from the roses | none of the plants survived | *the frost.* (2 marks)
    | the plants didn't survive |
    | no other plants survived |

Total: 11

Question 3 – one mark for each word or phrase between the vertical lines. Ignore the words printed in *italics*.
a *She was just standing there. It was* | as if/though she'd/she had (just) | *seen a ghost.* (1 mark)
b *By the end of the race, he* | had left the/all the other | *runners behind.* (1 mark)
c *The rain forests are vanishing. If we do nothing, by the year 2000 many species* | will have died | *out.*
(1 mark)
d *I was really hungry and the delicious smell* | made my | *mouth water.* (1 mark)
e *Would you be so good* | as to give me/us (etc) | *a lift (to the station etc.)?* (1 mark)
f *She is really looking* | forward to being | *taken out to dinner.* (1 mark)
Total: 6

Question 4 – one mark for each word or phrase between the vertical lines. Ignore the words printed in *italics*.
a *He shouted* | at the top of his voice, | *but nobody heard him.* (1 mark)
b *They asked the boss* | for a rise. | (1 mark)
c *It's about time* | we made a start. | (1 mark)
d *The roof needs mending,* | to say nothing of | *the walls and woodwork.* (1 mark)
e *The police car crashed* | while in pursuit of | *a stolen vehicle.* (1 mark)
f *I find it hard* | to make | ends meet. | (2 marks)
g *He* | took | great | exception to | *the story that appeared in the press.* (3 marks)
h *Which* | were the first | settlers to arrive? | (2 marks)
    | were the settlers | to arrive first? |
Total: 12

Section B
Question 5 – the mark shown for each question for coherent and relevant answers, not necessarily echoing the wording given here.
a so full of cigarette ends (1) that they are falling out (1)
b Hundreds of trees had to be cut down to provide the paper.   (1)
c the wine   (1)
d sprays a chemical (1) which is harmful to the atmosphere (1)
e in addition   (1)
f accelerates away very quickly and loudly (1); he adds noise to the other kinds of damage he does to the environment (1)
g a person whose habits (1) threaten the survival of the world (1)
h those who are concerned about the environment   (1)
i They no longer smoke, but Dank wants to do so.   (1)
j breathing in smoke (1) from other people's cigarettes (1)
k They refuse to drink Dank's wine (1), claiming to have stopped drinking red wine (1) or that they only drink at weekends (1).
l quickly drinks (1) his full glass of wine (1)
m renouncing the world   (1)
n Those who do so tell everyone whenever they can (1), strongly criticise people who have not done so (1) and consider themselves superior to them (1).
o One mark each for inclusion of the following twelve points, plus an impression mark of 0–4 for a well-expressed, cohesive paragraph, penalising irrelevance, indiscriminate lifting and subjective comment:
— little light in his home
— he smokes
— he drinks spirits
— he is unconcerned about tree preservation
— he drinks strong, possibly harmful wine
— he uses sprays which damage the Earth's atmosphere
— he uses a poisonous spray
— his car wastes oil/smears the road with oil
— his car pollutes the air with fumes containing lead
— he drives fast and his car is noisy
— he drops rubbish in the street
— he is not worried about his smoking harming other people's health   (16)
Total: 40

Paper 4: Listening Comprehension

1st part: **1 a** False   **b** False   **c** False   **d** False   **e** False   **f** True   **g** False   **h** False
($\frac{1}{2}$ mark each)
Total: 4
2nd part: **2** 1817 ($\frac{1}{2}$ mark), Intrepid ($\frac{1}{2}$ mark), 1860 ($\frac{1}{2}$ mark), Dutch ($\frac{1}{2}$ mark), tin and silver (1 mark), Chinese ($\frac{1}{2}$ mark), 1752 ($\frac{1}{2}$ mark), porcelain ($\frac{1}{2}$ mark), $15 million (1 mark), Portuguese ($\frac{1}{2}$ mark), gold and precious stones (1 mark), $8 billion (1 mark)
Total: 8
3rd part: **3** D   **4** a√   b   c√   d√   e   f   **5** C
Total: 5 (One mark for each correct tick)
4th part: **6** B   **7** C   **8** B
Total: 3